TO MOURN A CHILD

D1621873

TO MOURN A CHILD

Jewish Responses to Neonatal and Childhood Death

Edited by

JEFFREY SAKS

and

JOEL B. WOLOWELSKY

OUPRESS

Copyright © 2013 Jeffrey Saks and Joel B. Wolowelsky

To Mourn a Child: Jewish Responses to Neonatal and Childhood Death

Library of Congress Cataloging-in-Publication Data in progress

ISBN: 978-1-60280-233-9

Printed in USA

Typeset by Ariel Walden for Urim Publications

Published by
OU PRESS
an imprint of the Orthodox Union
11 Broadway
New York, NY 10004
www.oupress.org
oupress@ou.org

Distributed by
KTAV Publishers and Distributors, Inc.
888 Newark Avenue
Jersey City, NJ 07306
www.ktav.com

Contents

*T*hose who bury a child are forgiven all their sins.

— TALMUD *BERAKHOT* 5A

Foreword

Tzvi Hersh Weinreb

"THIS IS A GOOD book. I wish I had it long ago, at those times when I really needed it."

It is rare to have such a reaction to the books we read, even to those which we find interesting. But occasionally, we do come across books which we find practical and useful, and therefore wish that we had access to them at some important point in our past.

To Mourn a Child is such a book. As I began to peruse it chapter by chapter, I kept thinking of times in my professional careers and in my personal life when this book would have been a handy, and in some cases an absolutely essential, companion and resource.

As a pulpit rabbi and as a practicing psychologist, I have often encountered situations for which my training left me totally unprepared. The most powerful and poignant of those situations was facing parents who had lost their child. Others in my former professions are surely familiar with the temptation to avoid confronting parents in a state of grief. Yet, such confrontations are inevitable.

What does one say to a parent who is overcome by his or her emotions and feels that his or her world has come to an end? The difficulty of responding in such a situation is painfully compounded when the parent looks at the rabbi eye to eye and says, "You are the rabbi! You should have the answer! Why has this happened to me? Why has God taken my precious little treasure from me?"

Does Jewish theology have answers to such questions? Should those theological answers be provided to parents who are in the throes of grief? Which *halakhic* practices can be helpful to such parents, and which may be suspended in such tragic circumstances?

No less difficult is the position of the mental health professional who is asked to assist parents in coping with their boundless grief. What can be done to guide a bereaved parent through the tortuous stages of grief and mourning? How can one distinguish between normal reactions to tragic loss and pathological reactions which require special intervention? How can one assist others in the family, whether young siblings or aged grandparents of the deceased? What advice can we give to others who wish to help?

But it is not only the congregational rabbi or professional counselor who faces great difficulty in the encounter with those who suffered the unspeakable loss of a child. Every good friend and neighbor, colleague and casual acquaintance, faces the same difficulties. He or she correctly wonders as to whether anything should be said at all, and often fail to realize how helpful his or her very presence can be. What resources do such people have when tragedy strikes?

I especially remember the summer when I helped lead a group of bereaved parents as they spent an intense week together struggling to gain a perspective on the tragedies which beset them. It was the summer that the Jewish world learned about the horrible murder of young Leiby Kletzky, and reacted with such great compassion to his distraught parents. How ill-prepared I was, as were the other group leaders, for the reactions of the participants. Many of them felt resentful because so many thousands were moved by the plight of Leiby's parents, while so few even knew about their losses, which received no publicity and little attention.

How instructive it was to learn how some in the group were ready to abandon their faith in God, while others found their faith reinforced by their tragic loss. How important it was to learn about the therapeutic power of hearing from others who experienced such horrible pain, and how healing it is to know that one is not alone.

Not every bereaved parent has access to such group experiences. But with the appearance of this book, bereaved parents will also learn that they are not alone and that others, too many others, have walked the same sad path. Furthermore, the book will provide them with suggestions as to where they can turn for solace and consolation.

The editors of *To Mourn a Child* deserve the gratitude of the entire Jewish community for providing an invaluable resource for those who cope with loss and for all those who join them in their sorrow. They have gathered an impressive array of essays which, without exception, are literate, intelligent, and helpful, and which express the noblest ideals of the Jewish tradition.

The reader will find that, depending upon his or her circumstances, some of these essays will be of direct and immediate assistance, while others will be read with interest but seem less relevant. Be assured that those essays too will prove useful, perhaps indirectly, and perhaps on some future occasion. But each and every essay will be emotionally moving and spiritually edifying.

As Executive Vice President, Emeritus of the Orthodox Union, I am encouraged to see that the Orthodox Jewish community has been blessed with so many sensitive and articulate writers and thinkers of distinction.

I am proud that the Orthodox Union and its OU PRESS are making this volume available to our constituency and to the world beyond.

Together with all of humanity, I look forward to the day when "the Lord Almighty will wipe the tears off the faces of all mankind, and dispel death forever."

Introduction

Jeffrey Saks

A day-old child who dies . . . is to his father and mother and family like a full-grown bridegroom.

– MISHNAH *NIDDAH* 5:3

*K*ind people have said to me 'She is with God.' In one sense that is most certain. She is, like God, incomprehensible and unimaginable.

– C.S. LEWIS, *A GRIEF OBSERVED*

AS THE TITLE INDICATES, this volume addresses mourning the death of a child. Some of these essays deal with miscarriage or neonatal death, while others speak to the death of older children. Parents who experience such a loss are initiated into the unenviable fellowship of the *shakhul*, the Hebrew term reserved for the special category of bereaved parents. (See, for example, Gen. 27:45, 42:36, 43:14.)

While there are a number of other books that address both the general issue of mourning in the Jewish tradition and the special needs of the *shakhul*, we saw a need to gather between two covers a collection of essays that could be of comfort to grieving parents and offer insights to their friends and family members – as well as educators, rabbis, and other counselors – who glimpse the bereaved from what is surely another world. We included some well-known pieces as well as commissioning some newer voices in order to produce this anthology of reflections by parents on the loss of children from within a Jewish frame of reference, supplemented by writings of wise counselors on the experience of suffering such tragedies.

For myself, working as co-editor of this volume invoked the experience of watching my premature daughter die at but a few days old, and then navigating blindly and in isolation the emotional needs of mourning without the framework of *halakhic* ritual. The Bosnian-American novelist Aleksandar Hemon described the days of his daughter's final illness this way: "One early morning, driving to the hospital, I saw a number of able-bodied, energetic runners progressing along toward the sunny lakefront, and I had a strong physical sensation of being in an aquarium: I could see out, the people could see me (if they chose to pay attention), *but we were living and breathing in entirely different environments.*"

Looking through the thin glass pane of my own "aquarium" while numbly sitting in *shul* on the Friday night following her death, I wanted to shout out to those on the other side: "I had a daughter, her name was Neshama Chaya, she lived and died this week, she spent her whole short life in the NICU, and none of you will ever know her!"

Kind people tried to tell us from their side of the glass, "You're young, you can have other children," and this, thank God, proved to be true, yet entirely missed *half* the point. When parents lose a child, part of the grief is really for themselves – for however many months they anticipated the arrival, or for however many years they parented and watched them grow, so much of the parents' life becomes enwrapped in the anxiety and expectation connected with the child – emotionally, mentally, spiritually and even physically. With their death, the parents mourn not only the child, but their own lost expectations, hopes, and dreams as well. The idea that one can have other children is indeed a comfort. And yet, *that* child is gone from this world forever, leaving an indelible mark, and emotional scar, on the mother and father.

The Torah tells us that when Jacob is first reunited with Joseph after twenty-two years of believing his beloved son was dead, Joseph "appeared to him, and he fell on his neck, and he wept on his neck for a long time" (Gen. 46:29). Jacob's passive behavior during the encounter with his long lost son is puzzling – only Joseph is falling and weeping; what was Jacob doing? Rashi, citing the *Midrash Aggada*, suggests that the patriarch was occupied with the recitation of *Kriyat Shema*.

But another explanation is possible. The Torah doesn't state that Jacob wept, because it would be absolutely tautological to do so. We're not told that the father is crying now, because he's been crying for over two decades! "And all his sons and all his daughters arose to console him, but he refused to be consoled, for he said, 'Because I will descend on account of my son as a mourner to the grave,' and his father wept for him" (Gen. 37:35). When a child dies, part of the parent never stops crying, even as other parts may heal.

The *Shulhan Arukh* (*Yoreh Deah* 263:5) records that before a miscarried fetus is buried he or she should be given a Jewish name (and boys should be circumcised), and through this merit be remembered for resurrection in the World to Come. Another tradition records that giving a name will help the unconsoled parents recognize the child in the *Olam Ha-Ba*.

While my wife and I await that day, we see Neshama Chaya in our dreams and moments of quiet reflection.

"Those Who Bury a Child"

Joel B. Wolowelsky

"K*OVER ET BANAV*, THOSE who bury a child, are forgiven all their sins," says the Talmud (*Berakhot* 5b). This is not to say that children die because of their parents' sins. "The person who sins, he alone shall die. A child shall not share the burden of a parent's guilt, nor shall a parent share the burden of a child's guilt; the righteousness of the righteous shall be accounted to him alone, and the wickedness of the wicked shall be accounted to him alone" (Ezek. 18:20). Rather, it means that any punishment that might eventually be inflicted upon a person for their sins pales in comparison to the pain of losing a child. A person who experiences such pain is crushed and hence is "immune" from further punishment. One simply can't hold anything against them. "They are forgiven all their sins."

There are two blessings whose recitation is required upon hearing of the death of one's parents (*Berakhot* 59b; *Shulhan Arukh, Orah Hayyim* 223:2). The first obligation is well-known, the second more obscure. The "popular" *berakhah*, so to speak, is the *Dayyan Emet* blessing, which proclaims God to be the "True Judge." The second *berakhah*, the one whose obligatory recitation is generally not well known, is *Sheheheyanu* (or *Ha-tov Ve-hameitiv*), the *berakhah* which is recited when hearing good news or feeling great personal joy. What triggers the *berakhah* here is not the news of death, but the realization that one has inherited one's parent's estate! Whether riches come from winning the lottery or benefiting from

This essay is adapted from Joel B. Wolowelsky, *The Mind of the Mourner: Individual and Community in Jewish Mourning* (New York, NY: OU PRESS, 2010).

a life insurance policy, one is required to thank God. (As a practical technical matter, this *berakhah* is not usually recited nowadays, apparently because the current probate laws have created a reality where notice of death does not bring with it immediate inheritance. But that does not deny the basic truth it expresses.)

At first glance, we may admit, this *berakhah* seems a bit offensive. Surely this is not the time to focus on one's selfish reaction! However, the issue is not the inheritance, but rather the many selfish reactions death triggers. We worry about how we will survive financially; we sometimes are relieved of the burden of caring for a sick relative, and so on. These are not necessarily the noblest of emotions, and we might be afraid to admit them to ourselves, let alone to others. But the requirement to say this blessing expresses the necessity of bringing those internal responses to the surface so they may be confronted. When one has a secret too terrible to tell, it owns him or her. When the secret can be put out in the open, we learn to deal with it. If we don't like the way we are reacting, we can begin to work on ourselves. Requiring the recitation of *Sheheheyanu* does not endorse these feelings of selfishness but forces them to be acknowledged. Yet, says Rabbi Akiva Eiger (Gloss to *Shulhan Arukh, Orah Hayyim* 223:2), if parents inherit from the death of their child, *Sheheheyanu* is not said, as the death of one's child is a complete and unmitigated tragedy. There is nothing positive hidden in it.

Of course, there are those who have searched for an explanation of this tragedy, just as they have searched out other theodicies to justify God's actions. Alas, we can say of them that have not read the Book of Job. Indeed, if we had not read the first chapter, we might have thought that some or all the explanations offered by Job's friends for his misfortune, which included burying his children, were correct. The first chapter, then, is perhaps the most important of all those of the book. But having read the introduction to Job, we know that as good as those theories for his suffering might sound, they were not correct.

We do not get to read the "introductory chapter" of life to learn which theories are correct and which not. If silence is in general the correct posture in paying a *shivah* call, it is certainly appropriate for those who would comfort those who have buried their children.

TALMUDIC TRANSCRIPTS

It's hard to say what does constitute appropriate discourse for such a *shivah* visit. But it is instructive to listen in as the Talmud provides minutes of various inappropriate condolence calls. It should not surprise us that the Talmud records less-than-ideal rabbinic responses. The rabbis of the Talmudic period were the towers of our tradition; all that we do religiously stands on their shoulders. In showing them to have human frailties, the Talmud does not diminish them; it humbles us. If these giants could not always find the right word, we should not be so sure of our own abilities to comfort and explain.

One such Talmudic anecdote (*Bava Kamma* 38a-b) concerns Ulla, the fourth-century scholar who had at times traveled to Babylonia. The daughter of Rav Shmuel bar Yehuda had died and the Rabbis suggested that Ulla join them to comfort him. He refused. "What use do I have with these Babylonian comforters," he said. "They console by saying 'What can be done?'" He felt that such consolation was akin to blasphemy, as it suggested that they would change God's judgment if but they could.

Ulla felt that he had a more appropriate message of consolation to deliver, so he went by himself. The Jews were not allowed to wage war against Moab he said, because Ruth (from whom King David descended) and Nama Ha-Amonite (King Solomon's wife and mother of Rahavam) were to descend from them. If the daughter of Rav Shmuel bar Yehuda were righteous and worthy of having such worthy descendents, he explained, she surely would have been spared. God is indeed just.

In commenting on Ulla's message, Rabbi Shlomo Luria (*Yam Shel Shlomo*, number 10) notes that "what can one do?" is hardly blasphemy. It is nothing more than an expression of the fact that crying and excessive mourning will not bring back the deceased – something King David himself said when his baby son died: "While the child was yet alive, I fasted and wept: for I said, Who can tell whether God will be gracious to me, that the child may live? But now he is dead, why should I fast? Can I bring him back again?" (II Sam. 12:22–23). Moreover, R. Luria added, Ulla's comments are hurtful – and incorrect. It is often the case that righteous children die even though they were indeed worthy to have good things emerge from them. Better to comfort the mourners with talk of praise for the deceased.

R. Luria makes important points in his comments here. It is not simply that Ulla was wrong; it is that the purpose of condolences is not to present philosophical positions but to comfort the mourners. Moreover, he says, the fact that neither the Rif nor the Rosh quote Ulla's position in their *halakhic* summaries indicates that they reject it. The correct way to comfort mourners is to actually comfort them, not confront or lecture them.

This latter point was made strongly in an anecdote (*Avot de-Rabbi Natan*, version 1, chapter 14, abridged slightly here) concerning the death of the child of Rabbi Yohanan ben Zakai. The father was inconsolable and his students came to comfort him.

> Rabbi Eliezer said, "Adam had a son who died, and he accepted consolations. You too should accept consolations!" He replied, "Is it not enough that I must suffer from my own loss; must you also remind me of Adam's loss?!"
>
> Rabbi Yehoshua said, "Job had sons and daughters who all died in one day, and he accepted consolations. You too should accept consolations!" He replied, "Is it not enough that I must suffer from my own loss; must you also remind me of Job's loss?!"
>
> Rabbi Yosi said, "Aaron had two sons who both died in one day, and he accepted consolations. You too should accept consolations!" He replied, "Is it not enough that I must suffer from my own loss; must you also remind me of Aaron's loss?!"
>
> Rabbi Shimon said, "King David had a son who died, and he accepted consolations. You too should accept consolations!" He replied, "Is it not enough that I must suffer from my own loss; must you also remind me of King David's loss?!"

It is not surprising that none of these rabbis were able to comfort the father. What difference does it make if others could overcome their grief or if the "right thing to do" is to be consoled? They were properly rebuffed. Finally, Rabbi Elazar ben Arakh said, "You, Rebbe, had a son. He learned Torah, Prophets, the Writings, Mishnah, *Halakhot* and *Aggadot*; he died free of sin. You should be consoled as you returned whole that which was given to you for safekeeping."

Here was consolation directed to the father: You did well in raising him, he said. Nothing more could be expected of you. Your son was a wonderful person; he died free of sin. No wonder the father responded: "My son, you have consoled me the way people are indeed consoled."

Of course, as a matter of abstract philosophy, we believe that there *is* meaning to our suffering, that "God saw *all things* that He had made and, behold, it was very good" (Gen. 1:31). But the question is whether such a message can be heard by the mourner. Writes Rabbi Joseph B. Soloveitchik:

> Can such a metaphysic bring solace and comfort to modern man who finds himself in crisis, facing the monstrosity of evil, and to whom existence and absurdity appear to be bound up inextricably together? Is there in the transcendental and universal message a potential of remedial energy to be utilized by the rabbi who comes, like Zofar, Bildad and Eliphaz, the three friends of Job, to share the burden and to comfort his congregant in distress? We know that the friends of Job were not that successful in convincing Job about the nonexistence of evil. Can a rabbi be more successful? Can he succeed where the biblical friends of Job failed miserably? . . . . I can state with all candor that I personally have not been too successful in my attempts to spell out this metaphysic in terms meaningful to the distraught individual who floats aimlessly in all-encompassing blackness, like a withered leaf on a dark autumnal night tossed by wind and rain. I tried but failed, I think, miserably, like the friends of Job.*

We might well note yet another instructive anecdote (*Ketubot* 8b) regarding paying a *shivah* call to one who has buried his child. R. Hiyya bar Abba's son had died, and Resh Lakish went to comfort him accompanied by his *meturgaman*, Yehuda ben Nahmani. Instructed by Resh Lakish to say something appropriate, Yehuda ben Nahmani says, "'And the Lord saw and spurned, because of the provoking of His sons and daughters' (Deut 32:19) – in a generation which fathers spurn God, He is angry, and their sons and daughters die when they are young." Startled by the suggestion that appropriate comforting in such a case might include telling the father that the son had died in punishment for the former's sins, the Talmud asks, "He came to comfort and he grieved him?!"

Attempting to reframe these hurtful words, the Talmud then offers the explanation that Yehuda ben Nahmani was not accusing R. Hiyya of sinning, but was rather saying that he was important enough to be

---

* Joseph B. Soloveitchik, "A *Halakhic* Approach to Suffering," in *Out of the Whirlwind,"* pp. 99f.

held responsible for the shortcomings of the generation. Yet not every hurtful word can be withdrawn retroactively. It is interesting to note a contemporary reaction to this story. The father of a deceased eight-year-old girl would relate this Talmudic anecdote to those who were paying him a *shivah* call and ask, "How do you understand this Gemara? Is there comfort in losing a little girl for whatever transcendent reason?" The dead girl's grandparent added, "The question hung in the air like a heavy, dark cloud. I do not recall any answers that dispelled that cloud."*

While the death of a child requires special sensitivity on the part of the comforter, the unintended damage of misplaced comforting is not restricted to cases of a grieving parent. Rabbi Aharon Lichtenstein relates the following anecdote:

> Many years ago, I travelled to Bnei Brak to console my rabbi and teacher, Rav Yitzchak Hutner *zt'l*, in his mourning, when his wife had passed away. When I went to see him, I found him sitting alone. We had a private conversation, and this was conducted in a very open and honest fashion, from one heart to another. Rav Hutner told me that one of the *talmidei hakhamim* who came to console him tried to convince him and to "explain" to him how his wife's passing was "positive," inasmuch as she was now in the world of truth, a world which is entirely positive and other such nonsense. And indeed, it is not uncommon to hear such things when one goes to console a mourner, especially when the deceased passed away while being involved in a *mitzvah* or has fallen in battle, in sanctification of *Hashem's* name.
>
> It is superfluous to state that saying such things is totally unsuitable. I remember that when Rav Hutner told me this, he raised his voice and he applied the following severe words of the Midrash to that *talmid hakham*: "Any *talmid hakham* who lacks *da'at* is worse than a putrid animal carcass!" (*Vayikra Rabbah* 1). Rav Hutner added in his thunderous voice: "Did you hear this? 'Any *talmid hakham* who lacks *da'at.'* Consider this – we are not discussing an ignoramus who lacks *da'at*, but rather specifically a *talmid hakham*. A *talmid hakham* who has "filled his belly" with Talmud and the responsa literature, who is an expert in the *Ketzot HaHoshen* and *Netivot HaMishpat*. But if he lacks

---

* Seryl Sander, *Times of Challenge: Inspiring Stories of Triumph over Fear and Adversity* (Mesorah Publications, 1988), pp. 42f.

da'at which can direct and guide him so that he will act with understanding towards others and interact with them in a civil fashion, he is worse than a putrid animal carcass."

Had I not heard these incisive comments with my own ears from my rabbi and teacher, I would be fearful of voicing such sentiments of my own accord.*

One must come to comfort the mourners and not grieve them.

THE UNMOURNED CHILD

It is troubling to many that the death of a *nefel* (a baby who died within thirty days of birth) or a miscarried fetus carries with it no formal mourning, In these cases the parents are apparently deprived of the whole therapeutic mourning process available to all other mourners. To be sure, there is no denying that such a death triggers many of the same reactions as does the death of any relative. And, indeed, the absence of formal mourning is meant not to deny comfort and support but to protect the boundaries of human status.

Boundaries are an integral component of the *halakhah's* concept of holiness. Time is an uninterrupted continuum in which one instant is indistinguishable from the next. Yet Shabbat begins at a particular point. One second before, striking a match lights up a room; a second after the same act desecrates the holiness of the day. One can walk out of one's town on Shabbat and in one step that is indistinguishable from the one before it violate the holiness of the day by crossing the limits of travel outside one's city that is permitted on Shabbat. Similarly, the holiness of the Temple precincts and Jerusalem are defined according to their respective boundaries.

Human life is a continuum from the moment of conception to the moment of death (the exact time of which is itself a subject of debate). But only at a specific moment – "when its head emerges" – will the *halakhah* forbid it to be killed to save the mother. So, too, there is a moment when the *halakhah* assumes that the newborn is viable, the end of the

---

* Aharon Lichtenstein, "If There Is No *Da'at*, How Can We Have Leadership?" trans. Joseph Faith, available at http://www.zootorah.com/RationalistJudaism/DaatTorahLichtenstein.pdf

thirtieth day. Before that the death cannot be mourned as the passing of a full-fledged human.

A *shivah* call takes precedence over a *bikkur holim* visit to a sick individual, because the latter is a *hesed* (an expression of kindness) for only the sick person while the former is a *hesed* for both the mourner and the deceased. A *nefel* – and certainly a miscarried fetus – does not have full human status and so cannot be mourned formally. But the parents have not forfeited their right to the *hesed* due a suffering person. They are entitled to the same attention and support, albeit under the rubric of *bikkur holim* (visiting the sick) and not *nihum avelim* (comforting the mourners).

BIKKUR HOLIM

Kibbud (showing respect) requires formalism; we show respect by doing something that, in a sense, is illogical. For example, there is no real connection between standing up and showing respect; it is simply a formal gesture. We stand because there is no rational reason to do so other than to show respect. *Kibbud* requires well-acknowledged rules of behavior. *Hesed*, however, requires "only" compassion and its expression.

The respect that the community must pay a deceased person is done at the expense, so to speak, of the mourners' privacy. (For example, the door to the *shivah* house is unlocked and people enter unannounced and uninvited.) However, in the case of a miscarriage or the death of a *nefel*, the level of public awareness varies with each family, and the extent of public *bikkur holim* should reflect these differences. The same response will generally not do for both the case of an early miscarriage and that of a child who dies after twenty days in the intensive care unit following birth.

On a personal level, the most important reaction is one of expression of concern. "How can I help you?" is usually the most appropriate response. On a communal level, it is usually important to approach the mourner with a suggestion before implementing it. Here, too, options depend on what the concerned individuals would find appropriate. Some might find solace in a contribution to some charity; others might prefer a Torah class attended by friends; still others might find meaning in simply joining a *bikkur holim* group. The key is responding and not abandoning the people in pain.

The Death of King David's Son

II Samuel 12:15–23

THE LORD AFFLICTED THE child that Uriah's wife bore to David, and he became sick. David therefore sought God on behalf of the child. David fasted and went in and lay all night on the ground. The elders of his house stood beside him, to lift him from the ground, but he would not, nor did he eat food with them.

On the seventh day the child died, and David's servants were afraid to tell him that the child was dead, for they said, "Behold, while the child was yet alive, we spoke to him, and he did not listen to us. How then can we say to him the child is dead? He may do himself some harm."

But when David saw that his servants were whispering together, David understood that the child was dead. And David said to his servants, "Is the child dead?" They said, "He is dead."

Then David arose from the earth and washed and anointed himself and changed his clothes. And he went into the house of the Lord and worshiped. He then went to his own house. And when he asked, they set food before him, and he ate.

Then his servants said to him, "What is this thing that you have done? You fasted and wept for the child while he was alive; but when the child died, you arose and ate food." He said, "While the child was still alive, I fasted and wept, for I said, 'Who knows whether the Lord will be gracious to me, that the child may live?' But now he is dead. Why should I fast? Can I bring him back again? I shall go to him, but he will not return to me."

The Death of Rabbi Meir's Sons

Midrash Proverbs 31:10

RABBI MEIR SAT LEARNING Torah on a Shabbat afternoon in the House of Study. While he was there, his two sons died. What did their mother do? She laid them upon the bed and spread a linen cloth over them.

At the end of Shabbat, Rabbi Meir came home and asked her, "Where are my sons?" She replied, "They went to the House of Study." He said, "I did not see them there." She gave him the *havdalah* cup and he said the blessing for *havdalah*. Then he asked again, "Where are my sons?" She said, "They went to another place and they are coming." Then she gave him food to eat, and he ate and said the blessing.

Then she said, "I have a question to ask you." He said, "Ask it." She said, "Early today a man came here and gave me something to keep for him, a *pikkadon*, but now he has returned to ask for it back. Shall we return it to him or not?" He replied, "He who has received something on deposit must surely return it to its owner." She replied, "Without your knowledge, I would not return it."

Then she took him by the hand and brought him to the bed and took away the cloth and he saw his sons lying dead upon the bed. Then he began to weep and said about each, "Oh my son, my son; oh my teacher, my teacher. They were my sons, as all would say, but they were my teachers because they gave light to their father's face through their knowledge of the Torah."

Then his wife said to him, "Did you not say to me that one must return a deposit to its owner? Does it not say (Job 1:21), "The Lord gave, the Lord took, blessed be the name of the Lord"?

Suffering Infant Death:
A Multifaceted Experience

Steven Goldsmith

S UFFERING IS UNIVERSAL, YET each individual experiences a unique form of pain. The common questions of the sufferer include: Why me? How could *Hashem* do this? It doesn't seem fair? What about my *tefillot*? What does *Hashem* want from me? These questions relate to any type of distress, be it physical, psychological, social, familial, financial, etc. In one respect, the loss of an infant is one type of tragedy, which fits the mold of conventional suffering. However, in other respects, it is a unique experience, which features various forms of distress, which are specific to its circumstances. This essay will address these two elements, as they comprise the framework of my experience.

The process leading up to the death of our son was excruciatingly painful. In fact, it was more difficult to anticipate it, and to feel helpless in preventing it, than to accept the reality. Elyakim Chaim's death spanned a twenty-four hour time period from the beginning of his surgery until his passing. Those were the longest and most difficult twenty-four hours of my life. The *aninut*, which formally prevented my *tefillah*, coincided with physical and emotional exhaustion which left me with no energy to *daven* the next morning.

Throughout the hours of multiple resuscitations, and the ups and downs of our son's condition, I was wracked with guilt; sensing that if he died, the death would be my fault. I will never know the answer to that question; however, the agony and self-doubt was traumatic in its own right. I found myself feeling an exaggerated, hyper-intensive pre-*yom ha-din* feeling, nervous about the outcome. Such experiences should motivate *teshuvah*; however, the duress can project a distorted picture, in which the quality of the *teshuvah* is compromised, and its motivation seems superficial.

I remember *davening* a meaningful *minhah* during the surgery. I had reached an awareness and acceptance of the fact that *Hashem* could take my son away, and that I would have to live with that. Despite achieving that intellectual awareness, the car ride home from the hospital without Elyakim Chaim with us in his car seat created a tremendous sense of emptiness and loss.

During the *shivah*, we were comforted by family, friends, and even by people we didn't know, who had suffered a similar loss. Some offered deep insights, while others attempted explanations. We were open to listening to all of the words of comfort, because we knew that even if we did not necessarily agree, the words were spoken with good intentions.

My experience can be evaluated on two planes: The loss of Elyakim Chaim, and the conflict with *Hashem*.

Losing Elyakim Chaim was painful and depressing. I felt that I knew him so well; and yet, as he was nearly three months old, his identity was still undeveloped. In that respect, mourning over him related more to the loss of our connection, and less so to his unique self. I felt an intense closeness, and bond, to him. I greatly enjoyed his company, and dreamed of our future together: which activities we would do, what we would learn, and what we would discuss. His death left me feeling robbed of that future. However, after his death, I view his life as frozen and confined to that age.

Ironically, in the process of mourning, we try to reconnect through memories and pictures, etc. Yet at the same time, the healing comes through acceptance of that distance. Although I remember Elyakim Chaim's face when I see his picture; as time goes on, I have difficulty envisioning him from when he was alive.

The experience of infant death, perhaps like many forms of loss, casts a sense of doubt and insecurity about one's own life and the lives of the rest of his family. I was privileged to a meaningful conversation during the *shivah* with Rav Mosheh Lichtenstein. He, as opposed to many, did not try to soften the blow, but rather he attempted to articulate to the best of his ability the content and extent of my pain. He tried to get to where I was; as opposed to trying to get me to where he was. He recounted Rabbi Joseph B. Soloveitchik's description of the *Akeidat Yitzchak*. The Rav *zt"l* explained, *al derekh derash*, that when *Hashem* told Abraham to take Isaac, he emphasized that Isaac would not return. His death would not end on *Har Ha-Moriah*. *Hashem* emphasized: "You will wake up in the middle of the night, run to his room to check his bed, and he will not be there." The *Akeidat Yitzchak* did not only challenge Abraham in the present, but rather, it would bear the ramifications of loss throughout the future. This description was very meaningful to me. It captured the comprehensiveness of the experience; one tragedy impacts every other experience. I admit that I don't wake up and look for Elyakim Chaim, however I do have nightmares about infant death; and have exaggerated fears of tragedy befalling my family.

The loss also brought with it temporal discomfort. Social interactions became more complicated. I felt like no one understood where we were – and that they did not know how to relate to us. Some people tried to avoid me; others tried to distract me. Those approaches were not helpful. I don't resent them, because I know that they were afraid of saying the wrong thing.

Attending *semahot* after the *shloshim* was challenging. I felt that I could not connect to the joy in the air. Attending *britot* was very difficult, yet important. I would remember Elyakim Chaim's *brit*, especially if the current one was located in the same place as his was. Hearing the song *Zara Haya Ve-Kayama* (literally, "a prayer for viable children") elicited complex emotions. I prayed for others not to go through what we did; and yet in my subconscious there were pangs of imagining it happening to others. Those thoughts were very uncomfortable. It was difficult to look at other people's young children. It seemed as though things went so smoothly for other people. Ironically, despite the pain, I felt grateful for having such a profound introspective experience.

The experience of infant death is similar to general suffering when it comes to confronting *Hashem* after the fact. My experience was mixed with conflicted feelings. I felt: Why didn't You save him? How could You do this to him? Why did You do this to us? *Hashem* responded in silence. Yet, silence does not necessarily mean that one is being ignored. Rav Yehuda Amital *zt"l* explained that during the Holocaust, he felt *Hashem's* presence, he just couldn't understand Him.

I had difficulty reciting the blessing *Rofeh kol basar,* "Who heals all." What about Elyakim Chaim? I felt hurt. I had difficulty reconciling *Hashem's* decision to take Elyakim Chaim's life, while he was still granting me life, and yet I didn't feel that my whole relationship with Him could be dispensed with because of what had happened. I faced an irreconcilable problem. I could detach myself from the experience and revert to conventional service of *Hashem*, which is what I wanted to do, and yet I couldn't ignore the feeling of having been mistreated and attacked by Him.

I appreciated one piece in Rabbi Soloveitchik's *Out of the Whirlwind* in which he describes how man experiences *Hashem* on two different planes. Man experiences communion and closeness to God, yet he also experiences another form of Divine revelation through *Hester Panim* – God's hiding His face. Anger, distance, and detachment are not foreign elements to the religious experience, but rather are part and parcel of it. This was a crucial insight for me. Many people who suffer try to placate themselves by reinterpreting their suffering as good. In the process, they deceive themselves. They do this because they are too frightened to meet *Hashem* in such an uncomfortable territory.

In light of this point, I would like to add some of my own thoughts. Many people had recounted to me Rabbi Soloveitchik's approach to suffering, as expressed in *Kol Dodi Dofek*, that we ought not ask "why," but rather, "for what?" In other words: "What is the purpose of my suffering?" Thus, the sufferer is inspired to utilize his experience to reach new heights in *Avodat Hashem*. I agree that from a practical perspective the Rav's advice is sage and correct. However, I must humbly admit that I find a deficiency in this approach as well. His underlying assumption is correct, but does not take human emotion into enough consideration. Let me clarify. Objectively, *Hashem* is *tzaddik ve-yashar*, righteous and straight, all His ways are *mishpat*, they are just. However, it does not mean that emotionally one can always feel that way. Truth to tell, the sufferer often feels that *Hashem* is bullying him. Merely advising the sufferer to utilize that experience positively ignores the underlying conflict of both feeling anger towards *Hashem*, and yet believing that *Hashem* is compassionate, *hanun ve-rahum*. How can he utilize the experience to be a better *Eved Hashem* if he is disappointed with *Hashem*, and doesn't want to worship Him?

I believe that there is a response which is both twofold and self-contradictory. In my opinion, the sufferer must confront *Hashem* in *tefillah*; he must list his complaints and express his emotions honestly and respectfully. If he fails to do so, he is ignoring a gaping hole in his experience with *Hashem*. However, once he succeeds in expressing himself, he must detach. He must leave the mess where it is, and then return to the more positive elements of his experience. The negative feelings may inform a broader *hashkafah*, but that distance is better replaced with *devekut*, a cleaving to God. We cannot resolve the issue. *Hashem* is all-knowing and we are not. He expects us to be human and talk to Him as we would to others. However He also expects us to respect His Divinity, and our finitude. Thus, we must suspend judgment in abstract.

We say that everything that God does *letav avid*, He does for good. I believe that this does not mean that every cloud has a silver lining. Indeed, attempts to find the silver lining are often unsatisfying, misleading, and cheap. Many people cannot find a silver lining. I believe that *letav avid* is from *Hashem*'s perspective, not from man's perspective. *Hashem*'s definition of *tov ve-ra*, good and evil, is different than our own. It is legitimate for us to feel that it is *ra* from our perspective.

Despite my inclination to reject attempting to justify suffering in light of its positive educational value, I do believe that the experience of Elyakim Chaim's death gave Ariela and me the opportunity to grow in a number of ways. Often, I wonder why I couldn't grow by reading a book without having to deal with the pain. That decision was not given to me. Our experience has sensitized us to concealed pain. It has given us renewed appreciation for life; its finitude, and its value in the present. It has shaped the way we relate to our children, Akiva Nechemia and Yocheved Miriam, who were born since his death. We try to appreciate them in the present, and attempt to avoid the tendency to view an infant as undeveloped potential for the future.

I would like to conclude by noting that this description reflects my experience. I don't intend to claim that all similar sufferers do or ought to view the circumstances in the same light. I do hope that my account may help others who share similar sentiments, yet feel uncomfortable to express them, or who are looking for help in attempting to articulate them. May *Hashem* guide us in our quest to cleave to Him as He communicates with us through clouds of mystery, and uncertainty.

It's Never Too Late

Avraham (Avi) Weiss

GOD HAS BLESSED TOBY and me with three wonderful children: Dena, Elana, and Dov. We were also blessed with a fourth child born between Elana and Dov. His name was Yitzchak Rafael. It will be forty-years-ago this coming December that Yitzchak Rafael came into this world. He was affected with a dreadful genetic disease. He lived into his fourth month and then died.

Those days remain a blur. Toby and I were young, inexperienced, unable to handle this horror. And so my parents stepped in. They arranged everything including buying the burial plot for Yitzchak Rafael.

For a few years, Toby and I found it too painful to visit the grave. The time finally came when we felt ready to go. We called the cemetery and asked for the location of our son's grave. To our deep horror, the cemetery had no listing of a grave for Yitzchak Rafael.

We were frantic. We went to the cemetery to personally ask the staff if they had any record of Yitzchak Rafael's burial spot. They said no. We called the congregation on whose grounds we believed our son was laid to rest. They had no record of his grave. Perhaps, we thought, we had the wrong cemetery. So we visited all the adjoining ones – and still no Yitzchak Rafael. We were stymied, mystified and heartbroken. We were deeply pained as we had not put up a gravestone – the least we could do for our child.

Several years ago our dear friend Boris Stern, Roberta Horowitz' father, Bernie Horowitz' father-in-law, who sat behind me for years in shul, died. I accompanied the family to the cemetery and – lo and behold

---

Excerpted from a *Yizkor* sermon delivered in the Hebrew Institute of Riverdale, Yom Kippur 2010.

– it turned out to be the cemetery where I always thought Yitzchak Rafael was buried.

Something pulled me to approach the manager in the cemetery office. With my heart beating quickly and hands shaking I said, "I believe my infant son Yitzchak Rafael is buried here – could you check out his burial plot." The secretary went to the back of the room, returned several minutes later and said, "I'm deeply sorry but we have no record of a Yitzchak Rafael buried here."

"Would you mind if I check your records myself?"

"We don't usually do this," she said. Upset, I told her my story, how we could not find our infant dead son. "It's against protocol, but I'll make an exception. I'll allow you to check the record yourself."

I began going through the old records line by line. They had not been computerized and were hand written. Line by line I read the names aloud. And then I saw it. Yitzchak Rafael was not listed as Yitzchak Rafael Weiss but as Rafael Isaac Weiss. The child's dates of birth and death were beside his name. We had finally found our son.

That Yom Kippur, during *Yizkor*, right here, I resolved to put up the proper monument. But I didn't. I don't know why, but I didn't. On every subsequent *Yizkor*, I made the same resolution. You must do this, I said to myself. But I rationalized, it was almost forty years since his death, so much time had passed. Somehow, inexplicably, I just couldn't bring myself to make the arrangements.

This past year I became close to a gem of a person, a tzaddik named Joel Simon, who works at Riverside. One day, I'm not sure why, I told him my story. He embraced me and declared, "Let me help you put up the monument."

Yom Kippur is a time of *teshuvah*, of making amends. Is there ever a time when it's just too late? Is there ever a time when the statute of limitations has passed?

"It's never too late" is an adage that is easier said than done. First, it requires that the person making the amends be self-forgiving in recognizing that even after so much time all is not lost, *teshuvah* is possible. Second, for the mistake to be fixed it often requires assistance from others. And third, it requires a belief that even after so much time a gesture of genuine contrition will be accepted.

A story is told of Rabbi Yisrael Salanter, the father of the *Musar* movement. Once he went to a shoemaker to repair his shoes. It was late and dark. Noting the candle where the shoemaker was working was about to burn out, he said, "I'll return tomorrow and try again." "Do not despair" said the shoemaker. "As long as the candle burns I can fix shoes."

The message is clear. As long as there is light flickering, as long as there is a spark of life it is never too late. It is never too late to love; it is never too late to be in the formative years of life; it is never too late to engage in religious commitment and spiritual striving; it is never too late to dream, to do, to accomplish.

And while we pray the repair takes place in life, sometimes it can occur even after death. Maybe this is one of the meanings of *Yizkor*. Like the *yahrzeit* candle that many light for *Yizkor*, it reminds us that it is never too late even for those who have died, for whom we're saying *Yizkor*, to mend the fences.

There we were, Toby and I, just a few weeks ago at the gates of the cemetery where our son is buried. This particular cemetery is built with open paths, few trees, wide enough and open enough for a *kohen* to enter. We followed the cemetery map and finally came to the grave of our infant child. Most mourning involves remembering a person's past life; when one, however, loses a child, every day one mourns not what was, but what could have been.

But that day as we approached the grave, we were mourning our little child. He was still four months old. The grave was small, the gravestone tiny. It reads simple words:

פ"נ

הבן יקיר לי

יצחק רפאל – Yitzchak Rafael

בן טובה ואברהם חיים יוסף הכהן

December 3, 1970 – March 8, 1971

ו' כסלו תשל"א - י"א אדר תשל"א

We stood near the grave holding one another. We shed tears. Toby bent over to smooth the stone as if she was cleaning the room and making the bed of her little boy. I whispered to myself, "I love you Yitzi." And I am convinced I could hear Yitzi say, "It's ok, Abba. I love you too."

"The Only Way Around Is Through"

Yonit Rothchild

I T WAS TOTALLY UNEXPECTED. After forty-one-and-a-half weeks of a completely normal and healthy pregnancy, I went into the hospital on Saturday night September 22, 2001 to be induced the next day. That Shabbat had been full of excitement as my husband and I anticipated the arrival of our first child and our induction into parenthood. I went into labor on my own that night and had no problem progressing to the all-important ten centimeters of dilation by the next morning. Before I knew it, the final phase of pushing had begun. An hour and a half later I was still pushing and utterly exhausted, so I did not protest when our doctor opted for a C-section. At that point I just wanted to hold my baby. A few minutes later the surgery began. I did not feel any pain thanks to my epidural, yet I could feel pressure and tugging as the doctor worked on me. Even though there was a sheet screening my view of the surgery, I could tell when they took my baby out. But I did not hear a cry. "Something is wrong," I told my husband. He looked at me incredulously. "But they haven't even taken the baby out," he responded. After I continued insisting that the baby was out he looked around and saw a team of doctors crowded around what he knew was our newborn. There were shouts and commands for this medicine and that. A nurse told me to pray. It all felt like a horrible nightmare, and our worst fears were confirmed when a nurse told us that while the team had done everything they could, they could not save our son. That's how we learned that our baby was a boy, and also that he was already gone.

There was no explanation. No cord around the neck, no signs of anything abnormal, nothing. Later, tests on the baby and genetic testing on us would not yield any answers either. The only thing we perceived during those first few moments after our loss was a gaping black hole

41

of nothingness that was expanding by the minute and threatening to swallow us whole. As I rested in the recovery room I had my eyes closed tightly as I desperately tried to wrap my head around what had just happened while simultaneously attempting to block out all sights, sounds, and recognition of my reality. To my horror, the nurses brought me back to earth by suggesting that we might want to see and hold our deceased baby. It didn't take any thought for both my husband and me to quickly decline their offer. Aside from my trying to pretend that this was not really happening – could not be happening – it just seemed somehow un-Jewish to view and touch a dead body. My husband had anticipated that we would have to make decisions like this, so he had already called our local rabbis. Thankfully, it wasn't long before our first two visitors arrived.

The first two people to visit us were Rebbetzin Toby Weiss of the Hebrew Institute of Riverdale and Rabbi Jonathan Rosenblatt from the Riverdale Jewish Center. Together, they were exactly what we needed to find our way through those first dark hours. As soon as Toby walked in the tears came. It was as if the numbness knew to fade as soon as I had her support by my side. Her hugs and hand holding said more than a thousand words could say. Later, we found out that years earlier, Toby and her husband Rabbi Avi Weiss had also lost a baby. They were uniquely poised to help us through our healing, and they did. From bedside visits to sending us on a healing trip to Israel, they were there for us every step of the way. It's from them that we learned what a difference that kind of support can make, and because of them that we pass it on to others.

Rabbi Rosenblatt gave us the single most important piece of advice that we received during the whole experience. He explained to us very gently that there were two different ways to deal with our situation. We could choose to let the *hevra kadisha* handle everything. They would take the baby, give him a name, and bury him. We never had to think about our tragedy again and we could go home to heal. The other option was to be involved in the process in every possible way. To our surprise Rabbi Rosenblatt encouraged us to see our baby, to hold him, speak to him, and give him a name of our choice. This was not only permissible, he explained, but also preferable. Though more difficult at first, it would help us tremendously in the long run. Thankfully, we had the presence of mind to heed his advice, and that was the moment that our healing began.

One of the books that I was given about the loss of a baby had a repetitive image throughout. It was of a tree, full of leaves at first, then completely bare, and then fuller and fuller in every subsequent depiction as the book progressed. As the author intended, that tree provided me with a visual of our healing process and helped me believe that my own bare tree could possibly be full and vibrant once more. As it turned out, the decision that we made with Rabbi Rosenblatt's encouragement would dictate the pace and quality of our healing.

In the end, we did hold our baby. He looked absolutely perfect, just 'asleep.' It was then that I realized that the pregnancy and delivery were not a huge mistake at all, but had a purpose beyond my comprehension. We spoke to our baby and expressed our love. We accepted a memory box (which we had originally declined) prepared by the nurses which contained footprints, hair, and pictures of our baby. We named him Shalom Yair – "peace will light" – with the hope that this pure *neshamah* would somehow be a *melitz yosher*, "pure advocate," for the Jewish people and all of humanity who had just experienced the horror of 9/11. We had a small funeral during which my husband read a short eulogy. He implored our child to take refuge with King David who had also lost a baby. Rabbi Rosenblatt, who officiated at the funeral, explained to us that there was no need for that since our tradition teaches that God himself personally watches over and takes care of these tiny souls. We held an informal, non-*halakhic shivah* allowing friends, family, and strangers to share our pain and provide comfort. Slowly, the fog began to lift.

During those first days and weeks after our loss, I must have spoken to at least thirty women who had gone through similar experiences. Some were my parents' friends, others were complete strangers, and one was even my high school principal. I was shocked and also comforted by the knowledge that I was not alone. Each woman shared her experience of loss and also of healing, or sometimes lack thereof. I found that a stark pattern emerged. No matter when the loss occurred – within a few weeks of pregnancy, or a few months after birth – some women were able to heal while others had never really moved forward. The deciding factor was clear; those women who had confronted their loss head on were able to move on far more easily than those who were advised to, or chose to, push the tragic event away and sweep it under the proverbial rug. For the most part, the more a woman tried to shut out her loss, the more she became bound to it, while the more one let the experience penetrate, the easier it became to walk away. Those who tried to shut out their loss were still bound to it, while those who let it in were eventually able to walk away.

I heard many stories including an incredible recovery from the loss of a two-month-old infant and of the strength of a woman who had been pregnant eight times but had only one child. One woman told us how she and her family lovingly and joyfully honored the memory of their stillborn by holding the spices up towards heaven during the *havdalah* service when it came time to pass the spices around to each child in age order. Yet I also spoke to women still terribly haunted by their loss experience. I learned of a nagging sadness and regret from an early pregnancy miscarriage that had occurred twenty years earlier. I spoke to a woman who told me that when she had lost a baby towards the end of her pregnancy, she ended up secluded in her home and when she did go out, she felt as though she were wearing a scarlet letter A. My high school principal, then in her 60's, still regretted not holding her stillborn baby girl. I even received a note from a woman in her 90's, a friend of my grandmother, who regretted never giving her stillborn a name. Sometime later, I came across words that confirmed my experience. Words that I have passed along to many other people going through various kinds of difficulties. In one of the books that someone gave to me I read, "the quality of your grieving will determine the quality of your life." This sentence was followed up with a quote from Robert Frost. The famous poet once said, "the only way around is through."

For us, as I have no doubt it is for everyone else, the "way through" was not an easy path. It is laden with many tears. However, my experience has taught me that there is no other way to get out of the dark forest of grief. Even more so, I have found that there is a special light waiting on the other side. Suddenly everything in life is more vibrant than before. Nothing is taken for granted and everything is seen as a gift. Looking back now, I can understand the mysterious words of a stranger who called to comfort me when I was still in the hospital. She herself had given birth to a stillborn a few years earlier. She said, "that time period in my life is not a chapter that I would have chosen to be included in my book of life. But now that it has been written, it is not a chapter that I would take out either."

No one chooses to be the person that loses a baby, but we can choose the person we become because of our loss. We can choose to confront our loss and to learn from it. We can choose to become better people because of it. We can become better friends, sisters, brothers, daughters and sons. And if we are so blessed, we can become better parents to the children we have and those yet to come. There is no better tribute to the precious souls that we lost along the way.

The Faces of Anaelle

Brigitte Dayan Afilalo

CCORDING TO JEWISH TRADITION, a woman has seven faces in her lifetime. Our daughter, Anaelle Saada, experienced all seven in her 27 days. She looked different from one day to the next, sometimes from one morning to the afternoon. At times, she looked like a porcelain doll, with her jet black hair and white skin; other times, she looked a bit Asian, not at all from my belly; and once, she looked like a punk rocker with spiked hair. And always, her look lingered. She had dark, melancholic eyes that followed you with an intensity and focus uncommon to newborns. They exuded wisdom and vulnerability at the same time.

We learned to overlook her open chest, bloody from all the surgeries and procedures she endured, the IVs, the wires, the tubes. We came to see them as a natural part of her, almost believing for a while that they accompanied her from the womb. What we couldn't ignore were the numbers. The heart rate, the blood pressure, the oxygen saturation levels, the carbon dioxide, the hours we spent waiting for the doctors to come out of surgery, the minutes and then hours she seemed to be OK after each surgery, the freezing of time when she suffered each cardiac arrest. We came to watch those numbers with bated breath, feeling false hope each time they were stable, feeling anxiety when they vacillated, feeling that our world depended on the numbers on that monitor.

She took each surgery and each procedure with grace. But she humored us. She knew all along that she wouldn't stay, going along with the medical plan even though she knew it was futile.

They called the first surgery 'the repair.' Repair of the heart. They didn't call it a surgery. It sounded like we were taking a pair of pants to the tailor to get altered. Repair in Hebrew is *tikkun*. Could it be that she came down for a particular purpose, to accomplish something in 27 days and then return to her source? Whose soul did she possess? After the second cardiac arrest, I asked her to pray to her God. That she had a precious link with Him, I didn't doubt. She wasn't ever really ours, I told my husband. He bristled. "What do you mean?" he said. "How can you say that? Of course she was."

Biologically, perhaps. But not the same way her twin sister was ours. We never took care of her the way we did her twin. She baffled everyone, including the doctors, who never did figure out exactly what happened. She had a plan of her own, starting right in the womb, when she refused to come out after twenty hours of labor, prompting her sister to start the descent out of the birth canal, only to butt heads with her.

She had a timing of her own, Anaelle. We transported her to another hospital for an unanticipated surgery the first day of Rosh Hashanah. The Repair led to the Revision, as they called the second surgery, on Yom Kippur. Revision in Hebrew is *hazarah*. It also means repetition. Yom Kippur is the only day of the year where there is an extra *hazarah*, an extra repetition of the *Amidah*. Jews everywhere were invoking the mercy of the God who inscribes us for life and for death. We, too, were invoking the same God, but instead of words in the *siddur*, we mouthed numbers on the monitor. Our responsive reading: the doctors would read the numbers and we'd repeat them. "The blood pressure is in the 70's," they'd say enthusiastically. "The blood pressure is in the 70's!" we'd repeat enthusiastically.

We talked and talked to her. About our families, about how we met, about our values and how we planned to raise her and her sister. We'd joke, my husband and I, poking fun at each other in front of her, the way a couple might banter in front of company. We told her of our dreams, and we told her the details of our days. Holy and mundane. We converted that room into a happy place, conversing with the multitude of doctors and nurses about her medical condition and about their lives and our lives.

She had many names to match her many faces. Her first name: Baby A. It's how she was known to us and to the doctors throughout the pregnancy and the first three days of her life; her legal name: Anaelle Saada Dayan Afilalo; Chaya, meaning life, the name we added when her situation became critical; Poupee, meaning "doll" in French; my nickname for her. "*Poupee, poupee de maman,*" I'd say with a smile every time I walked into her hospital room. Many names, and several souls encapsulated in that body, my husband and I like to believe. An old soul that needed to finish something here on earth; perhaps someone from our family way back in Morocco. Someone who had unfinished business during the holy month of *Tishrei*.

"Why do you speculate?" my father, the ultimate rationalist, encouraged us not to think too much after her passing. "We don't know the answer, so better not to wonder."

We felt like puppet actors in a drama that was much bigger than we. It often seemed that we were watching the events happening to us from a balcony, participating in them and witnessing them but on some level, very helpless to influence them, like actors who don't have much influence on their writer. We were the main characters in this show, my husband and I and Anaelle. The doctors and nurses were the supporting characters; some had regular roles, some cameo appearances. Like on a television show, except that at the end of the season, we didn't shed our characters and there was no Oscar, for who can give a trophy to the writer known as God? And more importantly, the audience didn't like the show.

The last night, as I left the hospital, I tried to memorize her face. We had hope, but we had fear too. I was very afraid that I would forget her features, that they would somehow recede in my memory and that I would be left with a fuzzy image of her face. I lingered before leaving the hospital that night, trying to imprint every detail of her face and her body in my head, but trying to ignore the tubes and wires, like a mental PhotoShop. Her mesh of dark hair, her dark eyes, her little nose, her small lips, her triangular toenails, her fair skin. And then, with the story of the biblical Hagar in my head, who placed herself at a distance from her son Ishmael because she couldn't bear to witness his suffering and his death, I left the hospital shortly before she passed.

When I think of her now, it's not with the vivid details I studied that night. They seem less important now; we have photos of her for that. Rather, when I think of her now, I think of her aura, the aura of the baby who occupied the right side of my belly, the baby who came into the world for just a little while before returning to her Maker, the baby whom we are asking to be our angel up above and whom we hope is watching us with pride and with love, the baby who, for her short time with us, exuded the face of purity and innocence and wisdom and timelessness.

The Seventh Candle,
Which Will Forever Remain Unlit

Miriam Adahan

A JEWISH WOMAN USHERS IN the Sabbath by lighting candles: one for herself, her husband, and each of her children. Each Shabbos after I gave birth, it was an incredible joy for me to add an additional candle to the number I had been lighting. At forty, I finally had six candles, and I longed for more, for more light and more love. Since I had such difficulty getting pregnant, I treasured each of my children as a miracle. Each was different from the other; each was a whole world to be explored and developed. When my youngest was two, a miscarriage left me heartbroken. I just couldn't make peace with the idea of never having the arms of a little one around me again.

When at forty-four I discovered I was pregnant again, I felt I'd been privileged to return to that world of enchantment and joy which being pregnant always meant to me. Instead of my usual feelings of insecurity and vulnerability, I again felt tranquil and secure. I could actually feel the light of the *Shekhinah* surrounding me, protecting me. I would awaken each morning with a song of joy in my heart and go through the day, happy just to be alive.

From the time I was a child, I'd lived most of my life with a profound sense of isolation. More than anything, I longed to have a big, warm, close-knit family. But I married late, and after my first child, it took eight long years until the second came along. I loved being a mother, loved having a home filled with children, loved participating in their laughter as well as their woes.

At this point, with my only daughter about to leave home, and my

This essay originally appeared in *More of Our Lives: An Anthology of Women's Writings*, ed. Sarah Shapiro (Southfield, MI: Targum/Mesorah, 1991), pp. 151-57.

youngest boy soon to be away studying all day, I faced the prospect of an empty house with dread. So this pregnancy filled me with special delight. "I will not be alone after all!"

From the moment I knew I was pregnant, I sang and talked to "*Neshamaleh*," praying with her, sharing with her. My mind was filled with visions of holding a new baby and endless hugs and kisses. I didn't mind the excruciatingly painful varicose veins and disabling back problems. It was worth it to have a little body to hold, a face to smile into and eyes to smile back at me.

I felt like a teenager. I was in love with life. I was so grateful to my husband for having given me another child that I fell in love with him all over again. He was ecstatic, attentive and caring as if we were newly married. He kept saying how much more time he would have with this child now that he was older, what a special relationship he would have with a child born at a time when he could really appreciate it.

I was overjoyed for my oldest daughter. Now she would have a little sister somehow, I was so sure it was a girl, even before the ultrasound confirmed my belief. I had always felt badly that she had three rowdy little brothers and no sister with whom to share her thoughts and feelings. My own three sisters are such a source of comfort and warmth to me. Perhaps now she would feel more a part of the family and not be away from home so often.

And my boys, how excited and proud they were! How attentive they were toward me. They couldn't do enough to help. I imagined how a little sister would teach them to be gentle, to give of themselves. I kept imagining how we'd all laugh at her gurgles and her smiles and applaud her first words and her first steps. How we all needed a baby in the house.

All these years, whenever people asked me how many children I had, I'd always felt guilty saying four. I always imagined that they were think-ing "Only four? She took the easy way out! She has no right to talk about childbearing! She has no idea what it's like to take care of a large family! She doesn't even take her *frumkeit* seriously!" What I couldn't say was, "How heartbroken I've been not to have more children."

Those first few months flew by with such exhilaration. How proud I was when I finally put on my maternity clothes. No longer did the sense of isolation grip my heart with its icy fingers, hinting of the time when I'd be old and unwanted. There was a child with me at all times, a child I already loved with all my heart.

Things were perfect until I suddenly felt that the baby wasn't moving. I was gripped with fear. I dragged myself fearfully to the fateful ultrasound which confirmed my intuitive fear that my baby had died. I sat opposite the doctor in numb grief as I waited for him to tell me what to do next. I had never experienced pain like this before. Ah . . . so this is how painful it is to lose a child, one I've never even seen. Dear God, how do people go on living after losing a child they've already known and held? That level of pain was unimaginable.

I sat there and prayed: Dear God, give me strength to go on, to be loving and joyful again. God, if this is Your will, give me the strength to make it my will too. Let Your will be my will even though I want so desperately to have my baby back again. Let this loss bring me closer to You.

I didn't want to cry in front of the doctor. I was afraid he'd make the hurt worse by saying something flippant. So I saved my tears . . . for later, for the years that were in front of me.

And so began the long, painful process of again making *Hashem*'s will my will. It wasn't easy. All the pain of my life seemed focused on this loss. I wasn't ready to be old, to be thrown out of the land of the fertile. I grieved not only for the baby, but for my life, for my youth and for my childbearing ability. I struggled with the feeling of deadness, forced myself to get out of bed, make meals, clean the house, talk to people. But I was not really there.

My children found it difficult to bear my grief. They wanted me to be happy. So, when I needed to cry, I went into my room and sobbed by myself. Once, my youngest found me crying and he patted me on the shoulder and said, "Don't worry, Mommy, I'll be your baby." I smiled and hugged him tight. He was so precious. But he was five already, and I knew that in a short time, he too would pull away from me, as all children must. I missed the love and warmth that a baby would have brought, especially at this stage of life, when we have so much love and patience and wisdom to offer. It would have been so perfect. But my idea of perfect obviously wasn't God's. And God's will is what counts, not mine.

I found myself withdrawing from friends who were pregnant or had young babies. I kept trying to figure out what to do with the surprising degree of grief I felt each time I saw a pregnant woman or a new baby or saw a mother holding the hand of a little girl on the street. "Everything God does is for the best," I kept telling myself, but my heart refused to listen.

Night after night, I dreamed that I had given birth and had a healthy baby in my arms. She was alive. It had all been a mistake! I was so happy again. Then I would wake up and face the reality, and the tears would come again. I learned to be very stern with myself, commanding: "You must not be bitter or jealous! It is a *hillul Hashem*. Your children need to see a happy mother, a mother who is happy with whatever God gives!" I had to work so hard to internalize Torah truths.

Soon after, we moved next door to a family with a little girl who was born on the same day that my child had been due. Whenever I'd see her, I'd think, "This is what my daughter would be doing now." Then I'd command myself, "Don't stare, Miriam. Be happy for what others have. If God didn't mean for you to have this, then He knows what's best. Thank Him for all He has given you. There are so many worse tragedies that people go through."

Now it is five years and two more miscarriages later, and when I reach into the box of Shabbos candles at sunset, I still have to remind myself, "Six, not seven." Once in a while, I find myself imagining a sweet little girl with a big smile sitting with us at the Shabbos table with a pretty dress and a bow in her curly black hair. Each time, I stop myself sharply: "Discipline your mind, Miriam! Be only grateful! God only does good! Think only thoughts that make you feel closer to God, not more distant."

And I listen to the commands of my mind because I know that whatever God has given me is perfect. I know that growing older is something that can be done with grace and dignity. And I am ashamed of my self-pity when I hear of those who have lost mates, are childless, or have tragic illnesses. If I am to prepare myself for the future, I have to develop the special strength of a Jew, i.e., the ability to praise *Hashem* for whatever He gives us. The very word "*Yehudi*" comes from *lehodot*, "to be grateful." I am guilty of not being grateful enough. Perhaps my heart is a slow learner and I'll just have to be patient as I wait for it to catch up to my head. "Work harder," I order myself.

One Shabbos I went for a walk and met a friend who was strolling with her two little girls. "How come you're all alone?" she asked. I replied, "Because I don't have any little girls to walk with." I smiled to cover my sadness at being alone, but I saw a flicker of pain cross her face and felt bad. Silently, I berated myself: "It's not nice to make this sweet-faced, cheerful young mother feel bad. No one needs to know how you feel! Having four children is a miracle, not a tragedy! Have some emotional modesty, Miriam. You have no right to be sad! Most people have much more difficult lives. You're the one who teaches people how to accept God's will with joy, so get to work! God wanted you to produce books, not babies. Be grateful."

"I know, I know," I told myself. "I just forget sometimes. . . ."

Since then, I've discovered that many other older women, even those with very large families, have the same "just-one-more-child" wish buried in their hearts. Does the desire to create life, to hold a precious newborn in our arms ever cease? For some women, this is an eternal longing, part of what it means to be Chava, the giver of life. . . . Those of us with a strong urge to create and give simply have to find other ways.

I've always advised people, "Don't stew in the pain. Do something with it!" For me, my desire for more children is rooted in my strong need to love and be loved. So, I devote myself with new fervor to teaching EMETT (Emotional Maturity Established Through Torah), especially to helping young mothers create a loving atmosphere in their homes. Now that I've felt the sting of loneliness, I'm kinder to old people. We've "adopted" a Russian grandmother of eighty-two, who is quite alone in the world. Each Shabbos, we have Russian children from Chernobyl who are living in Israel without their parents. The more I give, the better I feel.

The mid-life crisis is waning. I'm no longer fighting the inevitable. I am getting used to not having any buffers between myself and the stark realities of life, such as loneliness and old age. The loss of youth meant crossing an invisible border and entering into a foreign land which seemed hostile and scary at first. Nothing prepares us for such losses except our faith in God and our bond to eternal values and beliefs.

When I didn't get what I wanted, I allowed jealousy and bitterness to take over my heart, even though, outwardly, I remained cheerful and full of *emunah* and *bitahon*. But one can't lie to God. Each time I said *Vetaher Libbenu*, "purify our hearts," I was very conscious of the need to purify myself from the feelings which were demoralizing me. The poison of jealousy and self-pity had infected me and it took strong doses of *Tehillim*, lots of prayer, and much Torah study to begin the healing process. Every once in a while, I would be rewarded with a glimpse of what a "pure heart" would mean: to feel tranquil and secure and totally accepting of my life as it is.

Everyone has a "candle" which will remain forever unlit. I discovered that making peace with the darkness is what brings light.

The Angels' Blessings

Joel B. Wolowelsky

WHAT CAN ONE SAY about this terrible ordeal which you have both gone through these past months? Anyone who tries to explain it and justify it is at best a fool and probably cruel. But I have always been taken with Rabbi Joseph B. Soloveitchik's view that while understanding evil and suffering is impossible, extracting positive lessons from it is not only possible, but obligatory. Indeed, perhaps the hardest thing for a person to do is to recognize the blessings that come hidden in suffering and to put aside the obvious and painful question of why these blessings could not have come free and clean. Framing our view of the past is the challenge of the moment.

There is no answer to this, but there is a thought to be drawn from the way we begin our Friday night Shabbat meal, a thought that occurred to me while saying *Shalom Aleikhem*. We sing this to welcome the two angels who accompany us home from shul. In Jewish tradition, angels are nothing more than divine messengers. Unlike humans, whose job is to grow and contribute, their job is simply to deliver God's message and then depart. Tradition says that these two angels have a blessing for the Jewish home, but they will not deliver it casually. They first accompany us home to see if the table is set, if the candles are lit, if the family is indeed ready for the blessing. When they see that all is in place, they deliver God's blessing with confidence and then leave. In singing *Shalom Aleikhem*, we welcome them, thank them, and wish them farewell.

These twins brought you great blessings. They forced you to confront and understand how important life is to you. They forced you to meet

---

Excerpt from a letter to a couple whose twin daughters died *in utero* after a difficult pregnancy.

tens of people with their own special messages. They gave you an opportunity to recognize altruistic giving, to appreciate the power that we all have — you included — to alleviate pain and enrich others. They gave you greater insight into the wonderful marriage you have. They exposed the power of Torah to mold a community and actualize its power. They challenged you to recreate what you gained in your approach to others.

There is no understanding the pain that accompanied them or answering the question of why these blessings could not have come without that pain. But when you sing *Shalom Aleikhem* each week, I hope you will remember the many blessings these two angels left when they saw that your family merited them. They delivered their blessings and departed.

We Will Get Better, We Must Get Better

Rookie Billet

MIRIAM RUTH

SHOUTS OF "*MAZAL TOV*! It's a girl! She's beautiful!" and she's right here near my heart and I close my eyes as the tears flow freely, because she is whole, and she is beautiful, and I thank *Hashem* for bringing me to this day, and for watching over her till birth, and I can't help thinking, *Hashem* — You've done Your job, and now You've entrusted her to me.

We name her after two grandmothers we knew and loved. Miriam and Ruth were not just names to us, but representative of the grandmothers who lived into our lifetimes, gave us beautiful times as children, and then were called from this world. I tell you all of this because you have to understand the utter joy and thankfulness I had been coming from when I suffered my loss. The tremendous joy and gratitude that I had felt upon her birth made the depth of my pain all the deeper at her death. So just as she began to grow, to fill out her small stretchies, to need a larger pamper, to smile at her *Ema* and turn her head at her name, she died, less than three months old, in her sleep. An unexplained sudden infant death, my beautiful baby.

In the emergency room they asked us — do you have a Rabbi we can call — and my husband and I looked at each other — because he is the Rabbi — we who had comforted others; now we were bereft. Amidst the terrible crying, the searing pain in the heart that felt like it would never go away, came the practical questions. How could we tell my parents, my

An earlier version of the first part of this essay originally appeared in *Times of Challenge* (Mesorah Publications, 1988).

husband's parents? How could we tell the children? What were we to do — we had to plan a funeral, a burial, a *shivah*, and then we would pick up the pieces of our shattered lives.

So many questions tear at the person who is suffering. What did I do to deserve this? I must be a terrible person. Why did this happen to me? May I be angry at *Hashem*? If I am angry at Him and I express my anger, will He only reach out to smite me some more? Why was this beautiful little soul denied a chance to live, to love, to learn? Surely she was completely pure. Then it must be a punishment to me, the errant adult.

As I return to the outer world from the inner one, I ask: How will I handle being the object of pity? How can I accept comfort when there is no comfort? I've lived a good and happy life. Can I ever be the same person I once was? Can I ever dance with a full heart at a *simhah*? Will every family photo from now on have that awful emptiness? Can I go back to the supermarket and walk down the pamper aisle without crying? Can I watch the peers of my baby as they grow from infancy to toddling to childhood to young adulthood? Can I run the risk of another child? Can I ever watch, handle, feed, someone else's baby?

What will I say when they ask how many children I have? I have three, but I had four. She existed; her life made a difference; how can I deny her? Yet can I burden an innocent questioner with my tale of sorrow? What shall we do with her clothes, her room, her untouched gifts, her little personalized picture frames and socks. Why didn't I take more pictures? Maybe it's better I have so few — maybe it's not healthy to keep looking at them and bursting into tears.

We make some decisions. We go home from the emergency room to tell the children. We tell them we love them. We tell them we can, we must, still be a happy family. We tell them we have suffered a terrible, irreversible loss, but no one is to blame. We all loved her so dearly and completely, and our pain is indescribable, but we will get better, we must get better. We will never forget her, but neither will her life, nor her death, be the center of our lives. There will be times over the next months when *Ema* or *Abba* will cry. That happens when someone we love dies. Crying is good — it helps us let out our feelings. We'll try not to cry too much, but if you kids want to cry, that's okay too. No, you will not die, too. Most people die when they're old. Some people die younger. When you die, your soul goes up to *Hashem*. Your body rests in the ground, in a grave.

We put a stone on a grave to express to ourselves and to the world who the loved one was and what he or she meant to us.

We're going to bury Miri here, but *al t'nai*. We're going to re-inter her in *Eretz Yisrael* before the *shloshim* is complete. *Ema* and *Abba* planned to be laid to rest in *Eretz Yisrael after* 120 years. You children will choose your own places. But Miri will never have a husband to be buried near. She only has us — and just as in life we would have tried to give her the best, in death, we will give her a fine resting place on a sunny hilltop in *Eretz Yisrael*, right next to where *Ema*, *Babi*, *Zaidy*, Grammy and Grampy bought their graves.

Another decision. Both *Abba* and *Ema* will say a *hesped* at the funeral. We will have a graveside funeral — simple — for a pure and simple soul. No one knew her as well as we — no one knew her as well as I. I speak of my love for her, of the death of potential, of not knowing what her first word would be, where her first step would take place. I speak of the way she looked at me as she paused in her nursing and I can see any mother who ever held and fed her child and experienced that simple social behavior imagine a little what such a loss is like.

The pain of the soul. The physical pain — from ending the nursing so abruptly. I cry and cry during *shivah*. Friends I have not seen for ages, reaching out as my head is filled with pictures of the baby. Talking, listening, trying to make people feel that they've comforted me, trying to reach every person who comes in with the message that his or her visit was appreciated, the visit served some purpose. Trying to find comfort from what people are saying. Trying to sort out the occasional stupid remarks and discount them. Wondering all the while what I will ever do when *shivah* is over.

The people, the troubles that crawled out of the woodwork. The incredible revelations of people who looked happy, looked elegant, gave charity, danced at weddings, yelled at their children. There were those among those who had also suffered, who had loved and lost, who had borne the deepest of pain. Could I too emerge from my pain and be my old self again, so that a stranger who had not known me in 1982 could meet me sometime later and not read from my countenance of what I had suffered? Could I possibly resume walking the streets of the world unblemished, without a sign of my loss, like an ordinary person? It seemed hard to contemplate, yet there walked those others, who, looking well and wonderful as they crossed the threshold of the mourners' house, spoke of the same unspeakable pains as I was feeling, but in the past tense.

For us, my husband and me, this was the beginning of a new understanding of *tzarot rabbim hatzi nehamah*, "the suffering of others offers a half comfort" — because we had asked ourselves: What can that mean? Why should I be comforted by the fact that others have suffered. Why would the suffering of others make me feel any better? The answer is that seeing those who have suffered, and who have also made a recovery, resumed their lives, survived, this is the *nehamah*! To see yourself a few months, years, down the road of life as you see those who have suffered and come back to a measure of themselves, this is the partial comfort. The knowledge that the road back from the loss can be scaled — it is not impossible — is the first inkling that there is a measure of comfort out there to be acquired.

Words that had meaning, words that gave comfort. The friend who had lost her beloved father a short time ago spoke of the question she found in a hasidic *sefer*. How will we recognize those we loved when we meet them after 120 years in the World to Come? If they died young, will they have grown old? If they were hurt or wounded, will they have healed? How will we know them, how will they know us if we have changed or aged? The answer is that we will know them, we will recognize them because they will be clothed and cloaked in the good deeds we do in their name. I could relate to this. I could see my baby come toward me in the World to Come draped with the *tzedakah* and *hesed* I would do in her name, we would all do in her name. I would no longer feel that half my life, or my whole life, for that matter, had been snuffed out. Now I would live for two. I would do all the good deeds and the *mitzvot* for myself, and I would also do the ones she had not lived to do.

I could appreciate the beautiful days fully, for her, as well as for me. I would dance on joyous occasions myself, but with an extra measure, for what she would have danced, had she lived. Through my life, I would give her life. There had to be some reason why she had lived, however briefly, why she had entered my life, and left it so abruptly, so painfully. And as much as I would sometimes feel, as a mother does, "*mir far dir*," a Yiddish expression that means if only I could go in her place, there was some unfathomable reason why I still lived, why I was still blessed with life. And I was going to use it, to cherish it, to live it as fully as I could.

Another friend mentioned the story reprinted in Rav Zevin's *Sippurei*

Hasidim of the baby born to a loving, fine, Jewish woman who lived two years and died suddenly. The mother went to the Rebbe who had given her the blessing for the child and he told her a strange story of a certain Jew who grew up to be an outstanding member of the community who, unfortunately, had been lost among other nations for several years during his youth. It was only through a special spark that this unique soul possessed that it was able to renounce its foreign background and return to Judaism. The story tells us that when this soul was reunited to its Maker after 120 years, *Hashem* felt that the soul, as wonderful as were the deeds it had achieved on earth, lacked one thing. For two years it had been nursed by a stranger. So the special beautiful soul had to return to earth, to a fine, caring Jewish mother, for two years. And this soul was her baby, the one that had lived two years and died.

I had never thought much about the transmigration of souls, but I understood that the teller of the tale was trying to tell me that mine, too, was a special home to which a special soul had been sent for a short sojourn, a small *tikkun* on its way to *Olam ha-Ba*. The storyteller wanted us to feel special at having been chosen. And though I found it hard to believe, in my heart of hearts, I said that stories such as these are not told without reason. I was happy I had nursed the baby almost exclusively, and I found a small comfort in thinking that perhaps there was something special about my baby's soul.

Another friend sent me the story of King David and his first child with Bat-Sheva. She reminded me of David's behavior while the child was ill. He wore sackcloth, he fasted, he prayed, he spoke to no one. Finally the child died. Everyone was afraid to tell David of the child's death, because if he had mourned so much while the child was still alive, while there was still hope, they feared for his life if he learned the child had died.

David began to realize they were shielding him. He asked outright and he learned that the child had died. To everyone's shock, he removed the sackcloth, got up, got dressed, and asked for something to eat. When the servants questioned him on his bizarre behavior, he explained, "While the child was alive, I prayed, I fasted, I humbled myself; there was still hope. Now that death has won this round, I shall go to him — he shall not return to me." And since David still lived, there was work to be done.

In the work of the poet Robert Frost, there are "miles to go before I sleep, / And miles to go before I sleep." And those miles must be covered through good deeds and good works. It was not so simple, however. I knew all these things in my mind. But to have your mind overpower the source of tears, to have your mind overpower the source of pain, to have your mind force yourself to greet your public, to go to school, to *shul*, to meetings, to business as usual, that is another thing.

There were times when I said to myself it would be easier to just have a breakdown — retire to a hospital for a month or two. But in thinking it through in more lucid moments I began to take a very practical attitude. What feelings, thoughts, actions, are productive, useful? And what feelings, thoughts, actions are wasteful and unproductive? Clearly, guilt is a very damaging and unproductive feeling. I was lucky. I knew I had been a good and caring mother. I had read in all the literature that Sudden Infant Death Syndrome, or SIDS, was neither predictable nor preventable and that I had nothing to feel guilty about because nothing I could have done would have prevented my baby's death.

And yet, the question remained. What if I had checked the baby earlier? If I had found the baby before it was too late, I could have begun CPR while there was still time. Like any mother, sometimes I had let the baby cry. I could feel guilty about that too. But I began to pull myself together and say: "Will it do me, my husband, my baby, of blessed memory, my remaining children and family any good if I devour myself with guilt? Will it help anyone in this entire world if I end up in an institution? Of course not. I had to do what was practical, what was valuable to the living. I had to get better. I had to discharge any negative, useless guilt feelings, and apply all my energy to being normal, being the kind of wife, mother, daughter, teacher, friend I always had been. I had to take charge of my life."

Shortly after I came to this conclusion in my heart of hearts, I came upon *Kol Dodi Dofek*, a wonderful essay written by the Rav, Rabbi Joseph B. Soloveitchik *zt"l* (my husband's rebbe) some years earlier and it crystallized for me in beautiful, poetic Hebrew the exact feelings that I had felt.* As I read it, I couldn't help feeling that my having thought of it myself cemented its meaning for me. Had someone external just told me about it, I might have said: "That's easy for you to say." But the Rav's words confirming my own thoughts gave me great strength.

In speaking of Job and the terrible *tzarot* that befell him, the essay discusses the age-old philosophical problem of "Why do the good suffer?"

---

* An excerpt from the English translation of *Kol Dodi Dofek* follows this essay – eds.

The Rav identifies two different kinds of personalities: *Adam ha-Goral,* "man of fate," is tempest-tossed by bad things, by troubles. In these brutal waves he is torn and battered as he goes whichever way the winds and storm blow him. *Adam ha-Yi'ud,* "man of destiny," is different. He too is tossed and battered by troubles, but he doesn't accept his fate passively. He gathers his strength and steers himself through, above the storm, and changes his fate into his destiny; he understands that his goal must be to change his fate into his destiny.

Other thinkers speak of individuals who changed their fate to their destiny, who did something at this point in their lives to say, "I must give meaning to this event by changing my life in some way." A friend of ours wrote a book he would never have written had he not lost the child. Another person told us how she got a degree in special education, thinking of the life she would have led had her SIDS baby somehow lived, and suffered brain damage. She wanted to give back in a meaningful way. I remembered the book by Martin Gray, a holocaust survivor, who lost his whole first family, married again, and then lost his wife and subsequent children in a fire, in which he tells of how he became active in forest fire prevention.

It was not clear to me at that moment precisely what I would do, but I think that from then on, I took charge of my life. I would go back to work. I would try to have another baby as soon as *Hashem* would give me the gift — not to replace, but to fill my empty arms, to respond to death with life. And I would share. I would have, unfortunately, over the next five years, many chances to give strength to families who lost babies. People would call and lead my husband and me to bereaved families. I would listen, I would speak, reflect and remember. I would call, I would be there, I would share. I would help them understand that their feelings were so normal. I would say aloud for them what they were afraid to say aloud, lest it be considered crazy or "out of sight" by the blessedly uninitiated.

I could tell them about how we decided what to write on her tombstone words that would help us say when we visited the grave, "Yes — that is what she was. This is how we felt about her." We wrote Miriam Rut bat Yitzchak Tsvi ve-Rahel, both father and mother, because we both felt the need to be joined with her memory through the stone. I would tell them how I put away the crib after *shivah,* how I packed the boxes of beautiful unworn gifts and wrote on them, "with mazel," as a mother who had lost a child to SIDS thirty years ago told me she did. I would tell them how I looked at her picture and cried, not wanting to torture myself, but somehow needing to.

I could tell them what others had told me in their turn — that the statement made at the end of the *shivah* call, "*Ha-Makom yinahem etkhem*," was not a wish, or a blessing, or a hope that the bereaved will be comforted, but rather a charge and a statement of irrefutable fact — "*Hashem* will indeed comfort you." Just as all those who have loved and lost before have eventually been comforted, so, too, will you. It has to be that way.

"I can tell you. I've been there. But you have to help yourself." "He who comes to be cleansed, the Almighty helps him." We have the concept of *hishtadlut*. We have to try. We are in charge of our lives, of our destiny. We have to spare no effort to put our minds in control of our emotions. If you desire it, it won't be just a fable — it will be real. If we will it, it can happen. And I believe in the power of the mind, of the intellect, to assess the situation and say — what is the best response? What is the response that will be most noble, most practical, most helpful to myself, to my family, to those I love and live for?

Once we decide upon that response, every fiber of our being has to go into implementing it. Even when I wake up in the morning and feel like going back to sleep for two weeks, I have to rise, dress, look my best, do my work, meet my public, get through that day. We are helped by talking things through with whatever network of support we have built for ourselves — a husband, a wife, a parent, dear friends, a trusted rabbi, doctor or therapist.

I was very blessed. I had a strong marriage, supportive parents and in-laws and good friends who helped to smooth the way. My prayers were answered, and my determination to respond to death with life was fulfilled. Before our baby's *yahrzeit*, I had a beautiful little son. It was a tension-filled time. There was so much riding on this child emotionally for both my husband and me.

We named him very significantly, we felt — Moshe Hillel, for the memory of our Miriam Ruth, of blessed memory. Moshe — because Miriam watched over her little brother Moshe in the bulrushes, and our Miriam would watch over Moshe from *shamayim* — and Hillel for our own *Hallel*, our rejoicing and thanksgiving, and because his *brit* was on Hanukkah and the complete *Hallel* is said each day, and also because we light candles each night in a pattern that is *mosif ve-holekh* — our light and our joy is multiplied progressively, as was the *pesak* of *Beit Hillel*.

We chose to have the baby put on an infant monitoring program which meant that whenever he was asleep, he would be attached by electrodes to a small machine, a monitor, that watched his breathing and heart rate, and would send an alarm if anything was irregular. For me, this was not a reflection of any lack of faith, or *emunah*, but an affirmation that I believed with a full heart that this child would make it. But I also felt that it was my responsibility as a parent to do the best I could. Just as I would always buckle my children's seatbelts no matter how short a distance I rode, I would always attach the monitor because I had to do my part — to use all the technology available to be a partner with *Ha-Kadosh Barukh Hu* to protect my baby and try to guarantee him life through my *hishtadlut*.

Every aspect of the baby's birth became a *déja vu* experience for me. In my mind I relived bringing home the baby that we lost, her first feeding, her first trip to the doctor. The first three months were the most difficult; my joy in him was tempered by the memory of my joy in Miriam and how that joy was doomed to be cut short so abruptly. And yet, the awe and wonderment and the profound gratitude for the great miracle of his birth was even greater.

When we heard during his naming at his *brit* , "*Zeh ha-katan gadol yihyeh*," and the blessing "*Kayem et ha-yeled ha-zeh le-Aviv u-le-Immo*," I cried very real tears, knowing that these prayers were not just words, but true supplications for life and longevity. But, the baby survived, his parents survived, and he brought a tremendous amount of joy into our lives. He did not replace, but helped to restore. To this very day we find him to be a special little boy with a *lev tov*.

The story doesn't end here. We were blessed with a little girl, whom we named Shira Naomi — also for Miriam Ruth — because Miriam went out and sang *shirah*, and we also wished to exult in our new baby girl, to sing *shirah*; and Naomi — for her love and devotion to Ruth. We had another little girl less than two years later, whom we were able to name without reference to the child we lost, which was also evidence of moving forward. I feel that these children have enriched our lives immeasurably. Our three older children still speak of the baby we lost and they have made her name familiar to the younger ones — integrating Miri's memory comfortably into the fabric of our family life.

Over the years we have given *tzedakah le-illuy nishmat* Miriam Ruth. My husband and I have delivered public *shi'urim* and dedicated them and other learning to Miriam Ruth and to the memory of other *kedoshim*. Our friends at the *shul* dedicated the *shtender* in the new *beit medrash* to the baby's memory. Although at first tears came to my eyes each time I saw the beautifully embroidered letters, *le-illui nishmat Miriam Ruth Billet bat Yitzchak Tzvi v'Rahel*, I can look at it now and feel that it is an expression of the love and empathy our friends felt for us. And an indication of our involvement in *Talmud Torah* for her, as I said earlier, an attempt to live for her as well, to do the good she did not live to do, and give meaning to her short life through deeds and study done for her sake.

Though the chapter is concluded, the story is not over, because the human mind is such that we continue to live with our memories. I am no longer cut to the quick by the thought of Miri, or the magnitude of what I lost, but I experience twinges of pain at different moments in life — on *Tisha Be-Av*, when we mourn the destruction of both Temples and the millions of children killed in those and subsequent holocausts — at the time of a family *simhah*, when people ask how many children I have, when I pray Rosh Hashanah and Yom Kippur and say "*mi yihyeh u-mi yamut*," and remember how I prayed on the High Holy Days that I was pregnant with Miri, little knowing that by *Shabbat Bereishit* I would have a perfect baby and after we read *Parashat Vayehi*, she would have died.

But I have lived with all of this. I also have a stronger recognition than ever before of how much I am blessed. I no longer try to think of what bad I must have done to deserve a *tzarah* such as this, but I gear my daily soul searching to being the best kind of person I can be. I don't believe that *heshbon ha-nefesh* should be geared to searching for the particular sins that might doom us to particular punishments. Our Sages tell us that rewards for *mitzvot* and punishments for sins are all settled in the World to Come. In this world we have to live a good and ethical life for its own sake. There is not a day that goes by that I do not say, Thank You *Hashem* for each day that dawns afresh in a beautiful world.

I have stronger intimations of my own mortality now than I had then; I am aware of what death is. I have seen it. I am still frightened of it, because of the great pain it causes the survivors. But I am less frightened at the prospect of my own death. I want to live long and fully, of course, but I am more sure that something awaits me after I have "crossed the bar." The death of my child has strengthened my belief that there is a World to Come. With our limited vision or narrow perception, we find it hard to imagine a world beyond our own world. But they exist, "Yes, I believe that there is a World to Come," cries the twin in the Journeys song "Conversations in the Womb."

So with what then, do I conclude? I have been struck, but I have survived. Losing a child is one of the most terrible and painful things that can happen to a person. And yet, the person who lives through this can still go to visit Israel and speak to family after family who have lost grown children, tall, beautiful sons whose potential had already begun to see fruition, and say: "I can put my own tragedy in perspective. Far greater *tzaddikim* than I have experienced *yissurim*, and the Talmud does speak about something called '*yissurim shel ahavah*.'"

Though the initial pain of my loss seemed to be unbearable, I have borne it. Time is also a great healer. Though the loss itself was irreversible, I have, thank God, three subsequent children who have been a source of enormous joy and who make life very full. We divided our family into the before and after. In jest, we called our first three children "the basics," and the last three, "the bonuses," for bonuses they are. Ours was not the kind of tragedy you continue to live with every waking hour. For this I am deeply grateful. I have walked forward, and I have not been smitten again and again, God forbid. My life, my soul, my self, my family, my relationships with people, my relationship with the Almighty, have all been enriched by Miri's life.

To answer the question I asked myself at the outset, "Could I ever again be the person I was before the tragedy?" I have to say, "Yes, I am the same person I once was, and yet, I am not. I can, once again, be happy with a full heart, as I never thought I would be able to be. But I have a different kind of vision now than I had then, a greater clarity of purpose, a more finely tuned sense of what is important, of how to help those who have suffered." There is much yet to say, but I'll stop here, and continue the conversation another time.

THIRTY YEARS LATER: REFLECTIONS ON A LIFETIME OF HEALING

Had she lived, the daughter that we lost would, at this writing, be in her thirties. The passage of time is a remarkable thing. There are still times I wonder what she would have been like, what profession would she have chosen, what would her talents be, what would her children be like, what a friend she'd be to me. . . . And yet, I feel like I am a whole person, someone who has been blessed with a good life. When I read the words I wrote twenty-five years ago about recovering from the death of a child, I still stand by them. But there are a few things that the years have added to what my husband and I learned from both the passage of the years and as a result of being called more times than we would have hoped to comfort other bereaved parents.

Perhaps the most important thing we learned is that just appearing at the *shivah*, or shortly thereafter, is truly important and helpful. Time and again, we were made to feel that our presence at the *shivah* house demonstrates to the newly bereaved parents that it is possible that someday they too will present themselves as we do – happy, healthy, productive people who have embraced life, who surely once felt as broken and utterly devastated as the recently bereaved parents do now. This very presence is a testimony to the possibility of life after loss. Speaking to the parents about the plethora of conflicting feelings of anger, guilt, helplessness, hopelessness helps them see that these feelings are not unique to them; they afflict all who suffer a loss, and they don't last forever.

At one *shivah* visit I made, the mother was comforting herself and everyone present by enumerating the "*hasdei Hashem*" that were inherent in her loss, in order to help herself feel that God was indeed with her, instead of allowing feelings of utter abandonment to prevail. She counted quite a few gifts: that the loss was her fifth child, and not her first, and that her house was still filled with the voices of children; that the death took place on *Erev Shabbat,* when her husband was home and she was not alone; that it was a child whose name she had chosen and not one that was named after a beloved relative, and so on. While these thoughts will not apply to every loss, and many may be too hurt or angry to benefit from such an exercise, the concept of finding the divine support even at a time that we feel most alone can be a helpful one.

I have long felt that healing is assisted by a mind that directs the heart to heal. Judaism supports the notion that the mind directs the heart; how else can there be commandments that say "do not hate your brother in your heart," "don't take revenge or hold a grudge," and "love the stranger" if they were not based on the premise that the mind can (and must) direct the heart. Similarly, even though Jewish law prescribes that formal mourning lasts for thirty days (except in the case of a parent), who is ready to cease grieving for a loved one after a mere thirty days? But the observant Jew is nudged to return to his life, to attend weddings and joyous events, because the healing process must proceed, whether or not the heart is ready. The grieving parent too, even though he or she may have experienced the most powerful of tragedies, must move forward and follow the prescription of doing the concrete acts that will propel the healing process.

Another point that may be helpful is to recognize the effect of the loss on the grandparents. I was keenly aware of this at the time of our baby's death. My parents and in-laws were devastated. I remember thinking how compounded their suffering was since they grieved for the child who would not live to adulthood, they grieved for their own children, the parents of the deceased, and they grieved for themselves. Moreover, the parents have the *shivah* context in which to be comforted, but the grandparents do not. The grandparents will often spend as much time at the *shivah* house as they can, and it is important for visitors to seek them out and offer love, respect, kindness and conversation.

This position became all too real to us, when eighteen years after our baby daughter passed away, we lost our Eliana Jacobson, the second child of our oldest daughter, a delightful, charming two-year-old who had filled our lives with joy. I don't think I ever believed I could be struck twice. Despite the fact that I knew people who had lost more than one son in the Israeli wars, and couples who had more than one Tay-Sachs child, I naively believed (or hoped) that bereavement guaranteed immunity from further losses. While I cannot in this context write in depth about the emotional journey that this second loss propelled, or how Dassi and Dan, the parents of Eliana, coped, it is important to note that despite the setback of this unfathomable tragedy, we and our family emerged from this loss as well. Once at a funeral, I heard a son speak of what a happy person his mother had been, despite having been a Holocaust survivor and having coped with illness, insufficient income and other challenges. He concluded saying that his mother taught him that "Happiness is more a function of disposition than it is of circumstance." I memorized the idea, because I am convinced that it is accurate. Finding happiness is not about being blessed with a set of wonderful life circumstances. Happiness is about cultivating within one's soul the capacity to be happy, to be positive, to be forward-thinking. I am reminded of Erich Fromm's theory in "The Art of Loving." He teaches that finding love is not about finding the right person to love, but about developing the capacity, the faculty to love. Hence, recovery from even the most horrific loss is a function of rebuilding one's positive disposition, one's capacity to have a happy nature, even when it seems impossible.

Finally, I must recommend not going it alone. Different people cope with loss in different ways. For some, friends and family will form a support network. Others will benefit from seeking the wise counsel of a sensitive mental health professional. Reading books and essays about how others coped with loss is helpful. Memorializing the loved one through charity and good works is a source of strength and comfort. Writing can be cathartic. Loss is an event that can profoundly affect a marriage; I have seen couples' marriages strengthened after loss, and I have also seen marriages dissolve in the wake of tragedy. It must be emphasized that while we do not have a choice about what happens to us, we do have a choice about how we confront what befalls us. May we have the strength and the blessing to face our most profound challenges with faith in the future, love, friendship, positive thinking and strength of character.

Fate and Destiny

Joseph B. Soloveitchik

CONSIDER: THIS WAS PRECISELY the answer that the Creator gave to Job. As long as Job philosophized, like a slave of fate, regarding the cause of and reason for suffering, as long as he demanded of God that He reveal to him the nature of evil, as long as he continued to question and complain, asking why and wherefore afflictions befall man, God answered him forcefully and caustically, posing to him the very powerful and pointed question, "Dost thou know?" "Who is this that darkeneth counsel by words without knowledge? Gird up now thy loins like a man; for I will demand of thee, and declare thou unto Me. Where wast thou when I laid the foundations of the earth? Declare if thou hast the understanding. . . . Dost thou know the time when the wild goats of the rock bring forth? Or canst thou mark when the hinds do calve?" (Job 38:2–4, 39:1). If you do not even know the ABC of creation, how can you so arrogantly presume to ask so many questions regarding the governance of the cosmos? However, once Job understood how strange and inappropriate his question was, how great was his ignorance, once he confessed unashamedly, "Therefore have I uttered that which I understood not, things too wonderful for me, which I knew not" (Job 42:4), the Almighty revealed to him the true principle contained in suffering, as formulated by the *halakhah*. God addressed him as a man of destiny and said: Job, it is true you will never understand the secret of "why," you will never comprehend the cause, or telos, of suffering. But there is one thing that you *are* obliged to know: the principle of mending one's

An excerpt from *Kol Dodi Dofek*, which appeared in English translation in Rabbi Joseph B. Soloveitchik, *Fate and Destiny: From Holocaust to the State of Israel*, trans. Lawrence Kaplan (Jersey City, NJ: Ktav Publishing House, 1992).

afflictions. If you can elevate yourself via your afflictions to a rank that you had hitherto not attained, then know full well that these afflictions were intended as a means for mending both your soul and your spirit. Job! when My lovingkindness overflowed toward you in the manner described by the verse, "Behold, I will extend peace to her like a river" (Isa. 66:12), when you were a prominent and influential person—"And this man [Job] was the greatest of all the people of the East" (Job 1:3)—you did not fulfill the task that My abundant lovingkindness imposed upon you. True, you were a wholehearted and upright man, you feared God and shunned evil; you did not use your power or wealth for bad; you dispensed a great deal of charity—"I put on righteousness, and it clothed itself with me: my justice was as a robe and a diadem" (Job 29:14)—nor were you ever loath to extend your help and support to the needy, but you came to their aid in times of distress—"For I delivered the poor that cried, the fatherless also, that had none to help him" (Job 29:12). However, in two respects you were lacking in that great attribute of *hesed*, of lovingkindness: (1) you never assumed your proper share of the burdens of communal responsibility and never joined in the community's pain and anguish; (2) nor did you ever properly empathize with the agonies of the individual sufferer. As a kind, good-hearted person, you took momentary pity on the orphan, you were very wealthy and could afford to give substantial charitable contributions without straining your financial resources. However, *hesed* means more than a passing sentiment, a superficial feeling; *hesed* demands more than a momentary tear or a cold coin. *Hesed* means to merge with the other person, to identify with his pain, to feel responsible for his fate. And this attribute of *hesed* you lacked in your relationships with the community and with the individual.

You were a contemporary of Jacob, who struggled with Laban, with Esau, and with the man at the ford of the Jabbok. Did you seek to help him and offer him of your counsel and wisdom? Who was Jacob? A poor shepherd. And you? A wealthy and influential man. Had you accorded Jacob a proper measure of sympathy, of caring, had you treated him with the attribute of steadfast lovingkindness, then he would not have had to endure so much suffering. You lived during the time of Moses and were numbered among Pharaoh's advisers. Did you lift a finger when Pharaoh decreed, "Every son that is born shall ye cast into the river" (Exod. 1:22), when the taskmasters worked your brethren with rigor? You were silent and did not protest, for you were afraid to be identified with the wretched slaves. To slip them a coin—fine, but to intervene publicly on their behalf—out of the question. You were fearful lest you be accused of dual loyalty. You were active during the generation of Ezra and Nehemiah and those who went up with them from Babylon. You, Job, with your wealth and influence, could have significantly accelerated the process of *yishuv ha-aretz*, of settling the land of Israel and building the Temple. However, you were deaf to the historical cry of the people. You did not storm and protest against the Sanballats, the Samaritans, and the other Jew-haters who sought to destroy the small Jewish community in Judea and thereby extinguish the last glimmer of hope of God's people. What did you do when those who went up from Babylon cried out, from the depths of pain and despair, "The strength of the bearers of burdens is decayed, and there is much rubbish; so that we are not able to build the wall" (Neh. 4:4)? You stood by idly! You did not participate in the struggle and suffering of those who fought for Judaism, for the land of Israel, and for the redemption; you never offered a single sacrifice on their behalf. You were concerned only about your own welfare, you would pray and offer a burnt-offering only on your own behalf. "And it was so, when the days of their [Job's sons'] fasting were gone about, that Job sent and sanctified them, and rose up early in the morning, and offered burnt-offerings according to the number of them all; for Job said: It may be that my sons have sinned, and blasphemed God in their hearts" (Job 1:5). Did you ever once offer a prayer on behalf of a stranger in a spirit of sharing in his grief? No! Don't you know, Job, that prayer is the possession of the community as a whole, and that an individual cannot approach the King and appeal to Him and present his requests before Him unless he redeems himself from his isolation and seclusion and attaches himself to the community? Have you forgotten that Jewish prayer is recited in the plural—"a man should always associate himself with the congregation" (*Berakhot* 30a), that Jewish prayer means that one soul is bound up with another soul, that stormy and tempestuous hearts merge and blend? You did not know how to utilize the formulation of prayer in the plural as fixed by the nation in order to include yourself among the many and in order to bear the yoke of your fellow man. Job, if you but wish to learn the teaching of the mending of one's afflictions, you must first apprehend the secret of prayer that brings the "I" closer to his fellow, you must first be able to recite clearly the authentic text of prayer whereby the individual partakes of the experience of the many, and you must first understand the idea of *hesed* as it is embodied by the prayerful person who rises above his individual uniqueness to achieve a sense of communal unity. You cannot discharge your obligation by merely dispensing a few clattering coins from amidst the abundant wealth with which you have been blessed. Only through a prayer fraught with the experience of a shared communal suffering will you be redeemed. You did not understand the teaching contained in lovingkindness and you frittered away the blessing which I bestowed upon you. Now seek to apprehend the teaching contained in suffering. Perhaps now you will be able to mend, in pain and grief, the sinful behavior you indulged in while in your previous state of self-satisfaction and pseudo-happiness.

God addressed the friends of Job: "Now therefore, take unto you seven bullocks and seven rams, and go unto My servant Job, and offer up for yourselves a burnt-offering; and My servant Job shall pray for You" (Job 42:8). Behold, I will test Job yet again. Let him be scrutinized publicly; will he now know how to pray for his fellow man, how to share in his suffering? Has he learned anything in this hour of calamity and wrath? Has he properly appropriated a new formulation of prayer which includes and encompasses the community? If he pleads on your behalf, then both he and you will be redeemed, "for him I will accept" (Job 42:8). Then you will know that Job has been delivered from the straits of egoism and has entered into the wide expanses of sympathy with the community and solidarity with one's fellow man, that his sense of detachment has disappeared and in its place a true spirit of communion has emerged. The great miracle occurred. Job suddenly grasped the true nature of Jewish prayer. In a moment he discovered its plural form, he descried the attribute of *hesed* which sweeps the individual from the private to the public domain. He began to live the life of the community, to feel its griefs, to mourn over its calamities, and to rejoice in its happiness. The afflictions of Job found their true rectification when he extricated himself from his fenced-in confines, and the divine wrath abated. "And the Lord turned the captivity of Job, *when he prayed for his friends*" (Job 42:10).

Reflections on Eliana's
Eleventh *Yahrzeit*

Dassi and Dan Jacobson

DASSI

H OW DOES ONE REFLECT on the loss of a child eleven years after her sudden death? I could reminisce about her beauty, her delightful personality, her adorable two-year-old sense of humor. I could remember the details, down to the minutiae, of the sunny day in June that she died. I could recall the days of *shivah* and the weeks that followed, the painful parts, the things that well-meaning people said that were inadvertently hurtful, and the enormous outpouring of love and support from dear ones as well as from strangers. Each of these could be an essay in its own right. For now, I choose to reflect on some of the things I have learned with the passage of time.

A decade is a long time. When Eliana passed away, Dan and I were still a young couple, married five years, with two beautiful children and one on the way, and we had work and graduate school and family occupying our time. I remember feeling after Eliana passed away that I had been living a charmed life, and that the clouds had come and covered the sun. I rejoiced in Teeli, our four-year-old first born daughter, in her chiseled beauty, in her cleverness, and we treasured her, fully understanding just how precious life was and is, and how easily a sunny morning can be transformed into the darkest nightmare. I worried about the unborn child inside of me. How would he be affected by the trauma I was experiencing, the uncertainty in body and spirit, and the upheaval in our family? Had I harmed him by taking one Xanax (an anti-anxiety pill) and two Ambiens (sleeping pills) in the two days after Eliana passed away, on doctor's orders, while I slept in my parents' house in my sister Nava's room with Teeli at my side, waiting for Dan to return from burying Eliana in Israel? Would my insomnia, lability, pain, worry, hypervigilance, affect the course of my pregnancy, or affect the fetus' development into a healthy newborn, at the right time? Mostly I worried about being able to be healthy and normal in my myriad roles as a person, wife, daughter, sister, friend, and especially parent.

When Eliana died, I was broken, we were broken, there was what seemed to be an unbridgeable hole in our family. Our extended family and many of our friends were broken right along with us. Many have told us they remember exactly where they were on that fateful day when they heard the news. I remember that one friend in an advanced state of pregnancy went into labor from the shock of what had happened. I recall the pain, and the despair, the dark days that followed Eliana's death. Most of our family and friends have heard me reflect that the day I got mad about something petty, like the politics of preschool or gymnastics carpool, I knew I was going to be OK.

But in order to get to the healthy place, where it's OK for petty things to be important, I had to learn some important lessons, some from conventional sources, and some from unexpected places. The first important lesson I learned from Dr. David Pelcovitz, child psychologist and expert in child trauma, when we went to consult with him about two weeks after Eliana passed away, trying to understand what to look for, was how to help Teeli, and how we would know if she needed more support than we could provide for her ourselves. There are a few things that still stand out for me from that meeting (strangely, I even remember what I was wearing), but the main important take-away message which has been with me ever since we sat with him in his office in Manhasset that day was the idea that everyone copes differently with loss, with bereavement . . . that there really is no "right" way to mourn a loss or to heal. David said to us, "You guys are both psychologists, you've already read all the literature." While that was clearly an exaggeration of the breadth of knowledge of the two graduate students sitting before him, it's not the important part. He talked about Elizabeth Kubler-Ross' stages of grief, and then he said: "You can throw it all out the window. Of course it's all meaningful, but it happens in a different order and a different way for each person." That was a critical lesson for me and for Dan as well. We were coping so differently, and it was frightening for each of us; my hysteria worried him: I think he was scared by my tearfulness and panic, and even may have wondered when he would get his wife back. I worried about him;

he who was usually so communicative appeared to be silent and stoic in a way that was terrifying for me. What would happen if Dan didn't find a way to mourn, I fretted. David gave us permission to not worry so much, to respect each others' different processes, because they were necessary elements to each of our healing. He also emphasized and reinforced the reassuring idea that we could be confident that if there was really something to worry about, we would know.

Another lesson came from psychiatrist Dr. Victor Fornari, also recommended to me for his expertise in trauma and bereavement. I went to see Victor after we had spent the summer in Israel, shortly before Roni, our third child, was born about four months after Eliana's death. Victor taught us the critical concept of before and after. In our initial meeting, he asked me what I was hoping to get out of therapy. I told him that I had come to see him primarily because many of my closest and most beloved were worried about me, and they were urging me to get help (the tears were still ever-present), but that I wasn't sure weekly treatment would be productive for me. I felt that I was "doing my life," and that things would hopefully improve with time, but that weekly focus on Eliana's death might not be helpful for me. I also communicated that my biggest concern, especially with a birth looming, was that Eliana's death would interfere with my functioning as a parent, and that the main goal that I would need conscious help achieving was to be a normal parent. Dan came in to meet Victor near the end of the session and when asked, he said he thought I was a little better than I had been in the immediate aftermath of Eliana's death, but I wasn't "back to normal." Victor said: "what normal? There's before and after, and that's it. You can be happy, healthy, life can be wonderful . . . but you can never go back." It was so simple and true – obvious almost – but for some reason stated like that, it helped us to envision the life "after." That was the final puzzle piece that helped me begin the journey back to life.

The next lesson I want to share comes from a surprising source, my favorite wizard, Albus Dumbledore, Headmaster of Hogwarts School of Witchcraft and Wizardry, with apologies to non-Harry Potter readers. (Parenthetically, I have found much comfort in the Harry Potter series in general, with the many layers of traumatic bereavement experienced by Harry and other characters, and with author J.K. Rowling's deep and insightful depiction of love, the process of grief, and coping with loss.) In the end of *Harry Potter and the Prisoner of Azkaban* (Book 3), for a short time Harry believes that his life was saved by his dead father. When he realizes that that is not what actually happened, he feels foolish, because of course his father couldn't save him, as he is, plainly, dead. Dumbledore delivers his wisdom, saying to Harry, "You think the dead ever truly leave us? You think we don't recall them more clearly than ever in times of great trouble? Your father is alive in you Harry, and shows himself plainly when you have need of him. How could you produce that particular Patronus [a spell that wards off dementors, evil magical creatures who suck out the human soul, leaving victims worse than dead]? Prongs [a boyhood nickname for Harry's father] rode again last night."

Harry's loss of his parents as a baby is obviously not the same as the loss of our two-year-old daughter. But there is so much truth in this statement. Eliana is always here, but not here, even after the passage of so much time. She is a part of who I am, who we are, and she is a part of our family. Her picture is displayed in our house, and our younger kids, though they never met her, make reference to her as their sister. When we moved into our house, and our older daughter Teeli set up her room, she chose to display just a few framed photos on her desk which were precious to her; one of the frames contains two pictures of Teeli frolicking with her little sister. The hole in our family exists still, though in some ways it has been bridged. Indeed, for me, Teeli's loss of her sister is perhaps the most enduring aspect of her death which cuts deep, especially as following Eliana's death our family has been blessed with four boys, but no sister-companion for my daughter. Knowing how much I value my relationship with my own sisters, now adults, despite a large age gap, I am more bereaved. But my mother says that my sisters, who are slightly closer to Teeli's age than they are to mine, can be her "sisters" as well, and others have said she will have friends who are like sisters, and as she grows, I see that both ideas are true, and I am comforted.

The final lesson is a lesson in love. It is not something someone preached to me; it is rather a lesson from life experience. The love and support provided by family and friends, colleagues and sometimes strangers who then became friends, whom I think of as "our support team," began eleven years ago and continues until this day. It is a gift to know how to communicate your needs, especially when the need is great. (When I counsel people who are bereaved, I tell them not to be afraid to communicate what helps as well as what doesn't help. The mutual benefit of assertiveness in the face of traumatic experience is immeasurable both for giver and receiver. It is hard to say, "Yes, I need this," but we will suffer more from not saying it.) In addition to our wonderful families, who provided love and support in every way, I am referring to people who hung out at *shivah*, some appearing multiple times despite a long car ride, a friend who spent her one week vacation before beginning medical residency taking Teeli places to give her relief from the crowds in the *shivah* house, friends who flew from Chicago, Boston, Baltimore, and even Israel to be with us during *shivah*. There were busy people who took from their own time to listen to us and speak with us, counsel us, even sing with us in a sad but meaningful guitar accompanied *kumsitz* one Saturday night in my parents' house. We were blessed with friends who provided us with a context to be in Israel for the summer and with mental health professionals who were always on call to help with any questions, including how to handle deep thoughts on death and burial from a four-, five-, or six-year-old. Sometimes a couple of years go by with no need to consult, but the relationships endure, and at each new stage, I know I can always call on them. There were those who fed us, called us, loved us, remembered the *yahrzeit* and Eliana's birthday every year, wrote *divrei Torah*, edited a whole *sefer*, asked the right questions, said the right things, or said nothing at all, and most importantly, stood by, watching, hugging, and loving us. Some of them don't even know the different ways in which they have touched us, but believe me there is no greater antidote to grief than love.

So where does that bring us? Back to that healthy place where we can afford to get angry over petty things. Thank God. To being normal, or at least trying to be. To appreciating life and trying to live each day to the fullest, to living the moments mindfully. To loving and also bickering with our children, to being normal parents. I am so grateful for the blessings of regular life. And for the blessing that we are able to stand up and strive to grow, strive to be better. We certainly experience life differently as a result of Eliana's death. If I could do a replay of a sunny Wednesday morning in June 10 years ago, I would welcome a rewrite of the script which left Eliana safe and happy and our family whole. Despite this, I know that we have learned and continue to learn the lessons of her loss, and we need to accept the curveballs of life, working, in the immortal wise words of Rav Joseph B. Soloveichik in his *Kol Dodi Dofek*, to turn fate into destiny.

DAN

A day after the eleventh *yahrzeit* of Eliana's sudden death at age two, I stood all alone in section five of the Eretz HaChaim cemetery outside Beit Shemesh. Nefesh b'Nefesh baseball hat shielding my head from the already intense early summer sun, welcome tears began to well up in my eyes. It was in the bright summer rays of Eretz HaChaim that I had found my "pool of tears" eleven years earlier, a month after the end of *shivah*.

One day in the middle of *shivah*, I sat in confusion and curiosity as two strangers from the broader community cried in front of me, telling me how utterly devastated I must be feeling. The problem was that, although I was deeply sad, I wasn't feeling devastated at all right then. After the accident, Dassi called to tell me that Eliana had been taken to the ER. I began the forty-minute drive home with tears in my eyes, screaming and bargaining with *Hashem*. By the time I arrived at the hospital, Eliana had passed away, and my intense emotions had simply vanished.

During the *shivah* and afterwards, Dassi was utterly lost, like a deer in the headlights. I was fully functional and abnormally normal given the context. During the weeks after *shivah*, I worried about Dassi . . . and she worried about me.

Why was I so stoic? Perhaps a classic "male out of touch with his emotions"? A psychologist by profession and a "people person," I was not normally one to be out of touch with my emotions. Perhaps, as a relative told me during *shivah*, "*attah yadati ki yerei E-lokim attah*." My stoicism was a righteous "*tzidduk ha-din*?" It didn't feel quite that way. Perhaps, subconsciously I knew that Dassi would need me to be her rock, so I "pulled it together"? In truth, I still don't know.

A month later, we departed for Israel with our four-year-old Teeli for a summer in Efrat at the NCSY *Kollel*; the outpouring of community love had been incredible, but we needed to "get away." Among others that we met with, we had a meeting with Dr. Yisrael Levitz, a senior psychologist who had taught me pastoral counseling at RIETS, to discuss handling traumatic bereavement. We shared with him our concerns about my state of emotional freeze. He responded that there is a pool of tears inside. Dassi had no trouble tapping into it – it was ever-present, but for me it was much harder. Dr. Levitz encouraged me to find ways to access the pool of tears near my heart, and told me that at the right time I would find it.

I had brought along with me to Israel an envelope received during *shivah* from a fellow graduate student; enclosed was a cassette audiotape of songs that she found inspiring and relevant. Most of the songs were *pareve*, but one of them somehow pierced straight through. With a sweet voice and a simple guitar accompaniment, a singer named Steven Curtis Chapman reached my pool of tears with his song "with hope": "This was not at all the way we thought it was supposed to be. We had so many plans for you, so many dreams."

Visiting Eliana's *kever*, I wanted to cry. In the still silence of the Eretz HaChaim cemetery, I stood out of cellphone reception, completely alone. I *davened* to *Hashem* for Eliana and for Dassi and Teeli. Strange as it felt in a cemetery, I turned on my music, "we go on with hope. . . ." I listened again and again, as my pool of tears finally released the pain, sadness, anxiety, and hope that had lain buried inside.

When tragedy strikes, the bereaved and comforters alike attempt to understand the state of the mourner. A month ago I sat with my American yeshiva students visiting an organization that services victims of terror. A speaker explained to us with definitive confidence exactly how the psychological process of bereavement works for a mother, and why it devastates her to the core. It was an interesting theory, but brought me back to our idiosyncratic responses to tragedy during and after our *shivah* eleven years ago.

Mishlei informs us that *"lev yodea marat nafsho."* Somehow we intuitively know how to find our way through our sorrows. Others can't necessarily dictate to us, and we can't always even understand our own reactions to tragedy. However, with time, patience, and *siyata di-shmaya* we each find our own path of hope.

Shivah In Yerushalayim:
A Letter To My Chana

Devora K. Wohlgelernter

February 12, 1986

W E BURIED CHANA PERE last night. It was dark and they had to use floodlights to see the grave. It was very dark. It made so much sense that it was night. I think God must have been so embarrassed that He wanted her to be buried in secret – when no one could see.

I remember that at your *Bat Mitzvah* dinner, I told you not to grow up too quickly. You will not grow up at all. I asked you not to make the clock go too fast; that I needed it to go slow. The clock has stopped. I told you to remain a child yet a while. You will remain a child in Daddy's and my heart until we join you.

I miss you. You are missing to me. My head aches from too little sleep and too many thoughts. I cannot sleep but maybe if I put some of the thoughts down on paper they will leave my head for a while. They are not bad thoughts. They are even good thoughts.

I have lived with fear and dread for seven years. But, in fact, I was never prepared. The doctors told us that if we were careful with food and insulin, you, Chanale, could lead a "normal" life. We were careful with food and insulin. Yours was not a "normal" life. How can two injections a day, having to eat when you are not hungry, waking up shrieking, resisting whipped cream from the age of five and pricking your fingers for a blood test three times a day be considered "normal"? Are they crazy? You cer-

Reprinted from *Tradition: A Journal of Orthodox Jewish Thought* 23:1 (Summer 1987), pp. 47–61.

tainly did not live a normal life, but, in fact, a supra-normal life. Let me talk about it.

You were my partner. My partner in crime. The rest of the family was naturally thin. I would gain five pounds just by looking at pecan pie. Or, so it seemed to me. We both looked longingly at all the cakes in the windows of the cafes on Yaffo Street. Last Thursday, when we were in town and had to wait for my eyeglasses to be ready, we went into a cafe. I ordered cappuccino and, for you, coffee with milk. The cappuccino had lots of whipped cream. You took a bit with your finger. I told you, gently I hope, to stop. You were not too upset with me, were you, my love? We cheated with a cinnamon bun. Half and half.

You were my partner in illness. Frightened more than the others. Understanding more than the others. When I was speaking to my friend Ruth on the telephone and telling her that I would need chemotherapy forever I did not know the door was open and that you were outside and heard. I found you sobbing. I thought I would die. What have I done, I thought. "It is not so terrible," I said to you. "Look, you will have to take shots for the rest of your life. Is that so bad?" "No," you answered, "that is not so bad." It wasn't so bad, was it, Chanale? But, wasn't there a peculiar glory in besting the illness for a while, my darling, Chanale? Were there not things you experienced simply because you had this illness? For example, take Camp NYDA (New York Diabetes Association camp). Your doctor said it would be good for you emotionally. It wasn't kosher, not even Jewish. "How can we send her?" I said to Daddy. "Just register her; then we will solve the problem," he said. We registered you. Then we went to the company that provided kosher food for the airlines and matched up meals with the camp meals. We brought the frozen dinners, together with kosher crackers and hotdogs, to camp. "Won't Chana feel funny being the only one eating kosher?" I asked the director, Al Passey. Al answered, "We have children allergic to wheat products, we have children allergic to milk products, so your Chana is allergic to *treif* (non-kosher food)." And we did it, Chana. I thought you should stay in NYDA for Shabbos; to leave would be disruptive. Daddy disagreed. "Chana must live with diabetes. Shabbos is part of her life. Therefore, Shabbos will just have to fit in."

And, so you quickly learned to give your own injections and we arranged to have you picked up just before Shabbos and taken to your sisters' camp an hour away and we had you brought back Saturday night.

You went with a pre-filled syringe, remember? That was before we trusted you to fill the syringe.

Did you fill it right last Sunday? Was there maybe just a bit too much insulin that tipped the scale? Did you look? Oh, my Chana Pere, how in God's name did you die? I must get back to NYDA. You loved it so. For three summers you spent a month not being different. Actually, you were different there too. You were the only one who got up early to *daven* (to pray), the only one who washed before eating bread and *bentsched* (said grace after meals). And how they respected you and loved you. You are the only one of my kids that went fishing and canoeing. You were a star in the production of Peter Pan. You are the only one of my girls who, at the age of eleven, was asked to be somebody's girlfriend. It just does not happen in our circles. I am glad it does not happen in our circles, but I am glad it happened to you. And you told him "no" because he was not Jewish; and because you were too young and your parents would not allow it. How we laughed when you told me about it. It felt good to be asked, didn't it? I am so glad you were asked. I have a selfish reason for having loved NYDA. It was the only time in the last seven years that I slept without listening for you with one ear.

February 10

Monday morning, 6:30 a.m. The children come to my bed. "We can't wake Chana," they say. There is a slight undercurrent of fear. I get up and get the glucagon. I inject. You were lying on your stomach. I could not see your face. I am sure the glucagon will work. I call Dr. Landau. "Call *Magen David Adom*, the Israeli Red Cross, and bring her to the hospital." "Ein Karem?" I ask. "Yes, I will be there." I call. I dress. I am very efficient. I have to be at Hadassah Ein Karem today for treatment. I know that you will be alright, that the glucagon will work. 6:55 a.m. *Magen David Adom* comes. They turn you over and start C.P.R. Your lips were blue, the color of gentian violet. Not Ein Karem. Too far. Hadassah at Mount Scopus. Five minutes away. The guy tells me to get the driver. They wire ahead to the hospital. "Get in the van." I get into the van. We come to the emergency room. They are waiting for you. I am sitting on a bench – trying to say *Tehillim* (Psalms). You are behind the curtain. I think they ask me something. I must have told them about the diabetes because I hear and see a nurse preparing to inject glucose intravenously. I telephone my sister Channie. "Come. It is very bad." "I will be there in 20 minutes." A doctor comes out. 'The situation is critical." "But not lost!" I say in a very determined way. "You must not give up!" "We won't give up," he says.

I realize now that he was just preparing me. That you had already died. That you were "dead on arrival," D.O.A. "Do you have family?" someone asks. "My sister is coming." Another doctor comes out from the curtained enclosure. "We did all we could," he says. It is 7:45 a.m. What is he saying to me? He looks very familiar. "You look familiar," I say. Now, I ask you, Chana Pere, wasn't that a ridiculous comment? He tells me you are dead and I say, "You look familiar." Well, you always knew you had a nutty mom. "I am Alon Moses," he says. Alon. Karin's son. Karin is the lady from whom I had let the beautiful house we are living in. This is not real. Aunt Channie comes. I have to see you. I go into the curtained room. I think the nurse was prepared for a scene. There was no scene. I just had to see you. You were lying there so sweetly. I closed your eyes which were slightly open. I kissed your face. Your lips were no longer blue. They were their usual pink. I moved the sheet a bit. There were blue lines on your body. Your beautiful little body. I could not bear to leave you. I kissed you again and again. How will I tell Daddy? He is in New York. How in the hell do you call a daddy and tell him that his precious child has just died?

Dr. Fink was in the hospital. I had met him 18 years ago in New York, soon after my marriage. I had been feeling absolutely dreadful. "I think I'm dying," I said. "No, you are just pregnant." Dr. Fink, head of the Emergency Room at Hadassah, Mount Scopus. He tried to get me through to an international operator. There was a social worker. Her name was Devora. He could not get an international operator. The telephone at the desk rang. It was for me. It was Daddy calling from New York. How could that be? He had called home to speak to all of you before you went off to school and the kids told him that I went to the hospital with you. So he called the Emergency Room. "What's happening, Deb?" he asked. "Yisrael, it has already happened." Was it a shriek I heard? A sob? A scream? It was the sound of a heart being broken in two. It was a terrible sound.

We made plans over the phone. He would pick up your brother Tati and try to get the first plane out. The nurse tells me that they have to take you to the *mekarer*. The refrigerator. My daughter to the *mekarer*? Are they nuts? No, they are not nuts. I tell her that I will go with you until the end. I learned eleven years ago when my babies died that you have to say goodbye. For eleven years, I have regretted not saying goodbye. I think that the nurse understood. I went until the *mekarer*. Imagine, my darling! I discussed Bubby (grandmother) and Zaide (grandfather) with my sister Channie and decided that it would be best if Channie would tell them and if they would come to my house to help me. Uncle Melech comes. Eighteen and one half years ago we called Uncle Melech from New York and said, "Uncle Melech, make us a wedding." That morning, I said, "Uncle Melech, make me a funeral."

Tamar and Yaakov Ross came. I was not alone. I came home. Channie was with me. Elisheva was home. She had gone to school but came home. I tell her. No matter how great my desire to record faithfully, I cannot record the look of horror, disbelief and pain. Dvarya comes in. How did I tell her? I just did. And, all the time I was thinking. How can I handle this without Daddy? And Daddy called to tell me that he could not get a flight right away and that, if it was easier for me, I should make the funeral without him. I know he meant it for my good but the thought horrified me. "Daddy deserves to be at the funeral of his beloved Chana Pere. Chana Pere deserves to have her Daddy at her funeral." And so, despite Yerushalayim pressure, we waited. I do not know how I passed the time. Yes, I do. I called the boys at the yeshiva where Daddy teaches and arranged for *shomrim* (guardians for the body before burial). Uncle Melech said we should have signs, so I got some boys from the Yeshiva to put them up. Aunt Channie slept over. How normal I acted. Chanale, I was half crazed.

February 11

I waited for Daddy. I don't remember what I did. His plane was supposed to land at 3:45. We set the time for 6:30. Daddy and I had decided to buy three plots on Har Hamenuhot, where Bubby and Zaide had bought plots. Melech and Miriam and Bubby and Zaide come to my house. I could not stay in the house. I waited in the street for Daddy to come. Uncle Moish had gone with Avraham Arych to pick him up. Uncle Melech told me to come into the house. I could not. Mena's Rebbe brought Mena home from *heder* (elementary school) and waited for Daddy. You would have loved Mena's Rebbe. We had decided that Mena should not go to the funeral but he had to see Daddy, so the Rebbe was waiting and then he would take Mena to his home. How can I describe what happened. Facts? Moish drove up. Daddy saw me. He got out of the car and took me in his arms. He was sobbing. I was sobbing. Perhaps there was some comfort in being together. I think there was. I am not sure. I think that in the days to come there will be. There always has been. We go to the funeral. Chanale, this is not real. Chanale, there were hundreds of people there. Hundreds. Uncle Moish spoke. He spoke so well. About you having been given to us as a *pikkadon*, a gift to keep for a while, and now the *pikkadon* is being taken away. And then Uncle Melech spoke. And then Daddy got up to speak. People tell me that they never heard such a *hesped* (eulogy). They tell me that it shook the rafters, that it was pure Picasso. I don't remember a thing. All I heard was one big scream and sob. All I saw was pain. As if pain can be realized into human form. I remember one phrase that he said, "*Rabbat banim umlala*, The mother of many is bereft." I will insist that he write the *hesped* down. I will help him.

February 12

It was Wednesday. It was our first full day of *shivah* (official mourning period). You know, my darling, during *shivah* hundreds of people came. You would think that we had lived in Yerushalayim for years. People come all day. And we cannot stop talking about you. The table in front of us is full of "you." The picture of you speaking at the *Bat Mitzvah* and that beautiful picture of you sitting in the chair at Rachel Rena's *Bat Mitzvah* party. You looked about seventeen years old. We show everyone the report that you had written on the thirty-nine *melakhot* of Shabbos (prohibited forms of work on the Sabbath). I brought it here so that I could show it to Bubby and Zaide. I was so very proud of it. Did you know that? I don't think so. But I don't think that it really mattered. You were very proud of it. Everyone who looked at it said things like, "A *yeshiva bachur* couldn't do better," or, "It is fitting for a first-year university student." No. Chana Pere, it was fitting for you. And we show them the book you made on the *Shoah* (Holocaust). And we show them the baby blanket you were sewing as a project in arts and crafts. And we show them the funny hat you made for Purim, just the day before you died. And your classmates come. In groups. They look as if they are in shock. We ask them to sit near us. We ask them to tell us about you. They speak in pain. They use words like *anavah* (modest), *mushlemet* (complete), brilliant, quiet. One girl says, "We miss the quiet in the class."

The day somehow rolled into the next. There is a night in between. When the last person leaves, it is late. Daddy sits and sobs out loud. I cry. I wondered if the children upstairs could hear. It was such a terrible sound. It is good that they heard. I cannot sleep. I write. The words sound hollow. I call my friend Ruth again in New York. Jacob tells me she is out. "Where is she? I have to speak to her." Jacob answers, "She is on the plane." My friend. The next day is the same. People keep coming. The neighbors bring food. I am part of a community. And then I begin to discover that we have become part of a club. The club of parents who have lost children.

You can tell them immediately. They do not sit in the back of the room. They come right up to the front and look you straight in the eye. Arlene and Alex Gross whose son Aron was killed in Chevron; Marion and Jason Propp, our friends from Petach Tikva, whose eleven-year-old son Aryeh was killed by an avalanche of earth while playing on a hill. The hill was just behind the apartment house we lived in when we were in Petach Tikva eight years ago. Sam and Judy Rosenbaum, whose son died of cancer, leaving a young widow and four small children. Rabbi Rose came. His son was killed while serving in Lebanon. Barbara Pomerantz, whose daughter died of a brain tumor. The Melameds, who lost a three-year-old daughter to cancer. The Falks, who lost a little son. And then there is Rabbi Dolgin, who came on Friday morning. I had never met him. He spoke of the fourteen-year-old daughter he lost twenty-five years ago to asthma. And, as he spoke, the tears rolled down his face and I found that I wanted to hear about this daughter. It was as if we were paying a *shivah* call to him twenty-five years later. He told us how they had sent her to Denver, Colorado, because that was the place for asthma patients and how the doctors had told him and his wife to take the child home because they didn't want her to die there. He told us how she had torn off all of the corners of the letters that she had received from friends and had stored them in a bag because they had written on them the letters ב"ה. He and his wife found the little sack that she had been keeping for *shemot*. Rabbi Dolgin's visit both comforted me and frightened me. I understand both the comfort and the fright. The fact is that Rabbi Dolgin has built quite a life in the last twenty-five years. That means you do go on. But the fact also is that he was crying on that Friday morning as if his precious daughter had just died. And I got a glimpse of what the future would be, and it frightened me. All of the members of the club said the same thing. Nothing will ever be the same again. I know it won't.

Chanale. I had crazy thoughts that night. That the club ought to have regular meetings. And that a good time for the meetings would be in the middle of the night. Because all of the members can't sleep anyway. And Daddy's brother Davy came and Ruth came and the neighbors kept bringing food. Do you know who else came? Reb Aryeh Levin's son. Can you imagine? I had read so much about Reb Aryeh Levin. He spoke of souls completing their mission. He spoke of *gilgulim*, the returning of souls to earth. And I listened and the words found their way. And we talked and talked and listened and listened. Your teachers came and we were hungry for their words. The private teacher told us how happy you were on that last Sunday. She told us that you were studying about the *Nesi'im*, Rabban Gamliel, Rabban Shimon ben Gamliel, Rabban Gamliel Ha-Sheni and Rabban Shimon ben Gamliel Ha-Sheni. And you told her that in our family we also had repeating names. Yisrael Elazar, then Yaakov Yitzhak, then Yisrael Elazar again, then Yaakov Yitzhak again. Let me speak about the private teacher. In the beginning, when we first came, remember how nervous you were about doing well in school? So, we got a private teacher. But, after three weeks, the teacher called to tell us how you really did not need private lessons, how you were already on the top of your class. When I mentioned to you the possibility of giving up the private teacher you were afraid. So I told you to keep the teacher. Let me stop calling her the "teacher." Her name is Miriam Eichler. I told you to call Miriam whenever you felt like it. That I did not want to be bothered with making or breaking appointments, that you knew your own schedule and I would settle the bill at the end of the month or whatever. And you gave me no argument. You accepted this gift with grace and with a smile. You did not give me a song and dance about how expensive it was or that you felt guilty because you really did not need it. You did not ask me twice or even once whether it was really alright. You just smiled. What a gift you gave to us. That you allowed Daddy and me to give to you. How gifted you were. It is something splendid to be able to accept a gift freely and with grace. This ability to receive a gift also gave you the ability to give. Do many people understand this? You allowed Daddy to go from shoe store to shoe store until you found the exact Shabbos shoes that you wanted. You were total love. And the mathematics teacher came and the science teacher. And they told us what we already knew but it was good to hear it. You are my daughter. Should I say you were my daughter? Are you not still my daughter? Will you not always be my daughter! Does death end it? I cannot feel that that is so. And then the teacher of Yiddish came.

And we found out that you went into a class with children that had been studying Yiddish for two years while you had never had an official class but that your longing for that language made up for lack of experience. You must have felt comfortable because you never complained. And your homeroom teacher who taught you Torah and Navi (Prophets) came. Chanale, you knew who you were and clearly all your teachers knew even though you were so quiet. *Shtiller heit.*

Day ran into day. All of Elisheva's class came, all of Dvarya's class came, all of Tehilla's class came. I didn't know that Tati had so many friends here. They all came. It seemed as if all Yerushalayim was crying with us. And then there was this man who came in and sat down. He had a long white beard. We did not know who he was. He said, "*Ha-Makom yenahem etkhem* – May God comfort you," and got up to leave. "Who are you!" we asked. "I am a Jew from Yerushalayim," he said. And left. Dr. Hersh came. Dr. Landau came and cried with us. "Why were we not warned!" we asked. She said so sadly, "And, if I told parents of every possibility, they would never sleep." And I think, my baby, that she was right. You did not live your life in fear. Diabetes was at most one big annoyance for you. And you even used it sometimes to have fun. Like the game "Dictopoly" that you and Elisheva made up. Patterned after "Monopoly," board and all. Instead of "Community Chest," you had "true" and "false" questions. Example: "You gave an injection in your leg this morning. You may not go skiing. True or False?" "You feel dizzy. You should drink diet Coke. True or False?" And instead of "Chance," you had instructions. Example, "You ate two chocolate bars. Go back three paces." "You learned to give an injection (we always called them shots) in your stomach. Hurray, go ahead five paces." You invented this game as a project in Manhattan Day School. Daddy and I were so excited. We spoke of patenting it. But we didn't know how to go about it. And then we were so busy living. And friends of Daddy whom he had not seen in ages came. Like Yisrael Weinberg and Duvie Hartman. "Do you remember," Duvie Hartman said to Daddy, "You were the one who got me to read when I came to Yeshiva University from Lakewood!" And Daddy remembered.

Why do I mention this, my Chanale? I really don't quite understand it myself. Maybe it is because that I found these echoes from the past comforting. That life is a continuum. That life is not made up of discrete (in the mathematical sense, i.e., separate) events, but that one event flows into the next and so, too, does health become part of the continuum.

Oh, Chana, I have to tell you about the wonderful people from Mena's *heder*. Mena's Rebbe, Rav Shraga Levy, Rav Miller, Rav Gamliel and especially for me Rav Deutch, the *Mashgiah Ruhani* of the *heder*. When Harav Deutch was here he spoke about how in the First World War many children died in *Eretz Yisrael* from sickness. He spoke about the concept of sacrifices, *korbanot*, for *Eretz Yisrael*. Daddy turned to me and said, "Listen Deb, you must hear this." And I listened but I don't think I heard. At any rate, I don't think that I understood. All night I thought about it. How terrible! Did my desire to come to *Eretz Yisrael* demand your death? And in the morning I called Rav Deutch and told him about my night and thoughts. He came over and we spoke for over an hour. He said that *has ve-shalom*, I should not think of *korban* as a sacrifice in this sense, and that in fact the years that were given to you were predetermined. But he spoke of another meaning of the word *korban*. A sign of acceptance – *ot hitratsut* – as with Abel. He also spoke of how the *mitzvah of* being in *Eretz Yisrael* is one of the three *mitzvot* that one does with the entire body, *sukkah* and *tevilah* being the others. I spoke about your love for *Eretz Yisrael* and your joy in being here. I am so glad that you were already a *bogeret* (adult in the eyes of Jewish law). That the *mitzvah* was truly yours. You know, my sweetheart, I feel as if I am talking to you and that you know exactly what I am talking about. Chanale, there is so much to tell about those "almost six" days. But I am so very tired.

February 18

This morning we got up from *shivah*. Last Monday, when our friends Emanuel and Jackie came, I said to them, "How will I sit *shivah*? I don't know how to sit *shivah*. I never have before." I must have sounded crazy. I did indeed sit *shivah*. But today it was over. Ever since last night, I have been fearing the end of *shivah*. What happens when *shivah* ends? Do we go back to normal? Do I go back to teaching on Mondays? Do I make a dentist appointment? Just like that? As if nothing? Do I laugh at a joke? Will I be able to laugh at a joke? And when we got up we went to the grave. That is the custom here in Yerushalayim.

It rained very hard on Friday night. When I started to *daven* with the *minyan*, Tati handed me my *siddur* (prayer book). In it was a note that he wrote. It said, "God is crying." Because of the rain the earth between the pebbles (do you call them "rocks"?) that they had put around the grave had sunk a little. It looked for real. Not pretend. Pretend. Do you know what the word "pretend" makes me think of, Chanale? How you used to put on a long dress, apron and the bonnet Dvarya got from Amish country and together with Tehilla (and the dolls, of course) used to pretend you were a character in "Little House on the Prairie." So sweet. So sweet. I can almost taste the sweetness.

I looked at the grave and knew that your body was lying below. I knew because I saw the *hevra kaddisha* (burial society) put it there. And they were dignified and gentle. Why does that matter so much to me? Because it does. We came home. The mood was angry. Daddy does not speak to me. In all of our other troubles, I always felt that we became bonded more strongly. But this is a different order of magnitude. Any touch between us is painful. How unhappy I am! That sounds ridiculous. You are gone from me and I say "How unhappy I am!"

Later in the day, Rabbi Dovid Kaminetsky, the principal of Manhattan Day School, telephones. He tells me how your class is grieving; so many had just received letters from you and had answered immediately. He tells me that your class has elected to study *Mishnah Rosh Hashanah*. He tells me that he had sent some letters from the students to me and is surprised that I have not received them. The minute I hang up, Uncle Moish walks in with the mail. Among the letters was one that Rabbi Kaminetsky had pulled from your file. It was a letter that I had written to the school in February 1982, giving detailed explanations to the staff on how to handle emergencies. I write, "We are trying very hard to raise an independent, unspoiled kid, who does not view herself as an invalid. Since the burden she bears is so heavy (shots twice a day and a restricted diet are no picnic) this is sometimes hard because one is tempted to treat her with silk gloves." We did not treat you with silk gloves. You were angry at the disease but I think I can honestly say that you never felt sorry for yourself. You reacted violently to any special consideration. You honestly felt that there were so many worse things. You felt bad when a sister was unhappy in school, especially since you were so very happy. You felt bad if a friend did not have any brothers or sisters, thinking how much luckier you were despite the fights.

You were capable of a compassion that I have never seen in anyone. No kidding! When Ophir, our new friend, was getting married and his parents refused to come because they were angry that he had become a *ba'al teshuvah* (an observant Jew), you were so upset and insisted that we all go to the wedding. Daddy was in New York. It was on a Monday night. Less than one week before you died. I cannot believe it, my *ziskeit* (sweetness). And you wore my black wool dress and the necklace we had given you for the *Bat Mitzvah*. I told you how beautiful you looked. And we went. The bride was so pretty and Ophir was so happy to see us. As we were leaving, you kept saying to me: "Mommy, promise me that we will keep in touch. Promise me." And I promised you. Ophir and Einat paid us a *shivah* call. In the letter that I had written to Manhattan Day School in 1982, it also said: "I realize that I am asking everyone to invest some extra time in this child but I can promise you that she will do the Yeshiva proud." Rabbi Kaminetsky reminded me of that line and said in his letter: "Today, I can honestly tell you that this is certainly true. She has made us all very proud because of her love of Torah, her beautiful *middot* (qualities) and her very pleasant disposition despite the fact that she had to deal with a very difficult illness." Oh, my baby, you were so, so pleasant and I miss you. So, so much.

February 19

We have just returned from an *azkarah* (memorial service) at your school. I dressed nicely – just the way you would have wanted. I was a pretty Mommy. I wanted my Chana Pere's Mommy to be pretty. The children and the teachers from the upper grades were all there. Ruth and Channie went with Daddy and me. Chanale, I have no words. The principal spoke of your love of the Book of Jeremiah; the homeroom teacher spoke of how you touched the lives of so many even though you were only in the school for such a short time. The assembly was held in the gym and birds had flown in through the windows. They were chirping the whole time. I like to think that you were watching us all and laughing at the birds. It was really as if they too wanted to talk about you, my sweet child. And then some children spoke. They read poetry they had written. They spoke of pain and of the anguish at not being able to have said good-bye. They spoke of ache and of God. What beautiful children they were! One would have thought that you had been at the school for years and not just five months. The children recounted things they had heard in our house when they came during *shivah*. One girl remembered that I had told her of your desire to have a calisthenics class and my difficulty in finding one for you. And then on that last Sunday, Aunt Channie gave me a number to call. I did and was so happy to find someone who was organizing a class for girls your age. I went on and on telling this woman whom I had never met how thrilled I was and how thrilled you would be. She was going to call me on Wednesday to tell me of the final arrangements. I told you and you were so happy. I find myself being grateful for so many things, Chana Pere. Like being able to tell you about the calisthenics class before you died. The girl at the *azkarah* also told everyone that Daddy had told her of your desire to marry a Gerrer Hasid. She told everyone about the card that Daddy had sent you from London with the picture of the Grenadier Guards with their fur hats and belted uniforms. "How would you like to marry this type of Hasid?" Daddy wrote to you. "He is also wearing a *gartel* (Hasidic prayer belt)." The postcard came on Thursday when we were sitting *shivah*. How you would have laughed! The student also re-membered how I had told her about that time you were at Dr. Ginzburg's and she said, "I understand Chana." And you pounded the desk with your fist and said, "You do not understand!" How can someone who does not have diabetes understand someone who does? And we would speak that perhaps some day you would be a juvenile diabetes doctor and when you would say, "I understand," it would be true. And then Daddy spoke to everyone. You would have been so proud. He spoke of true *hesed (hesed shel emet)*, the *hesed* that one does for someone who is no longer living, the kindness that cannot be repaid. And he thanked all of the children for their coming to us and sharing their impressions. And he said that this was a true *hesed* to you, my Chanale, but also to us because we hope never to have to repay this type of kindness. And then he spoke about the *sidra* (weekly portion of the Torah), *Tetzavveh*. And he spoke of the fact that Moshe Rabbenu's name is not mentioned in the *sidra*. He told the children that *Hazal* (the Sages) say that this was because when he was praying for the people in *Parshat Ki Tissa*, he said, "If You will not spare the people then erase me from Your Book." And that even though his motives were pure and, in fact, his prayer successful (God did forgive the Children of Israel) one has to be very careful with what one says. And he told everybody, Chanale, how he never heard you say anything against anyone, how all your words were naturally measured and gentle. Did I take you too much for granted, my angel? Did I tell you enough how special you were? Did you know how much pride we took in you? And then Daddy spoke about the verse from the Song of Songs, "Your eyes are like doves." And he told everyone how beautiful your eyes were and deep.

And then he told them what *Hazal* say about the dove – pure and gentle. And everyone was so quiet. You would have been very proud of Daddy. Even without the *beckeshe*, the Hasidic garb. When we came home and I started to write, I looked for your *Bat Mitzvah* speech on a diskette. All during *shivah* I could not find it. And I found it today. You spoke about the Book of Ruth and how you were accepting upon yourself all the *mitzvot*. The last sentence is, "'I want to die in *Eretz Yisrael*,' Ruth declared. 'And there I will be buried.' For *Hazal* tell us that being buried in *Eretz Yisrael* is like one who is buried under the altar." I could not believe my eyes. I must stop for a while, my darling. The computer is getting wet with tears.

February 23

Sunday morning. Ruthie left for the airport. Elisheva, Dvarya and Tehilla have gone to school. Daddy went to *daven*. Tati, too. Temima is waiting for Daddy to take her to *gan* (nursery school). Mena has a fever. He had a dream last night. That you were very sick and we thought you were dead so we buried you but then you got better and broke through the box (there was no box, but he is dreaming) and came home. It is getting worse. I keep looking at your pictures and the things you wrote. I try to find comfort in the fact that everything I read and see shows me that there was much joy in your young life. Whom do I weep for? You? Me? Me and Daddy? We cannot stop crying. I look at the family picture from your *Bat Mitzvah* and think how we were sitting on top of the world that evening. I cannot imagine taking a family picture again. Something has happened to the children – I mean the older ones. Especially Elisheva and Dvarya. I know this sounds crazy but they seem more tranquil. Happier with themselves. I think that I understand it. I think that they have seen what the loss of you has done to Daddy and me. I think that they sense that it is terrible and irreparable. Oh, my God, words simply cannot say it. And I think that they realize how valuable a child is and how valuable each of them is. I am talking to you. Like I always have. Like my little friend. We so often spoke of how the older ones were not as happy as you in school and with themselves and that this was the reason that sometimes they would pick on you. I have to believe that you are watching us and seeing this transformation. I imagine you coming to me quietly and saying, "Do you see, Mom? It makes me happy."

I don't know how to end this letter to you. I am tired and my bones ache. "Lie down, Mommy," you would say to me. Maybe you still are saying it but I cannot hear you. I long to hear you. I love you, Chanale. I miss you. You are missing to me. I cannot bear it.

February 24

It is a Monday. Exactly two weeks since you died. I did not think that I would write anymore. But I have been thinking and I have to talk to you some more. I think about that last night a lot. I dwell on the details. On that last Sunday night I took off your glasses (you were falling asleep studying) and kissed you goodnight. You were happy. Confident in the next day. Yesterday, I received a letter from Gord. Remember? My college friend from Chicago. Her real name is Esther Friedman but I have always called her Gord. It was a beautiful letter. She writes that I must consider myself blessed that "her short years were filled with rich and varied experiences. Imagine, to be one of seven children. On the one hand to be a litte sister and, at the same time, to be a big sister. To be blessed with parents whose life styles brought the whole family into contact with a broad spectrum of people and whose outlooks were open, inquiring, and at the same time, firmly rooted in Torah. To live in Manhattan and walk out, past the doorman, into the hustle and bustle of the 'Big Apple' on the way to a school and a community in total contrast to the style and content and culture of 101 West 12th Street. To straddle both worlds and to dream eagerly of reaching the best in both." Yes, Chanale, we were and are very blessed. I do not remember ever having angry words with you except about matters that concerned the diabetes. (Did you eat enough? Did you take a blood test? How I hated those questions. You did, too, I know. But I had no choice. Please, my darling, forgive me.) Daddy and I have only sweetness and joy to look back upon. Do you know what Temima said the other day? She said, "Chana is in *shamayim* (heaven) playing with *Hashem* (God)." And do you know what Mena said? He said that we must take all of your notebooks and put them in a bag and save them to give to the *Mashiah* when he comes so that he can give them to you.

I am writing this on May 22nd. It is exactly one solar year since Chana Pere's *Bat Mitzvah*.

And then Chana died. Period.

The sentence stands by itself. There doesn't seem to be anything to put before it or after it.

Just . . . And then Chana died.

I go to the grave. I don't want to go. I want to go. I am fearful of going. I simply must go. I like to go alone, without Yisrael. I am not sure that I understand why. The day before yesterday we went together. He put his arm around me and we wept. I must learn to go to the grave together with Yisrael. I think that when I learn to do that with ease, there will be something to put after the period. We buried Chana on Har Hamenuhot – the mountain of rest. It is one of the many mountains that surround Yerushalayim. The grave is down the slope and looks over the rolling hills. You cannot see any buildings. I stand at the top of the steps and look down at the grave. It never seems real to me. The tombstone stands out among all of the others. It is white and shining in the Yerushalayim sun. The monument is stately. Even as I write I have this surrealistic feeling. Can this all be true? Is my Chanale really dead? Will I really never see her again? We went shopping for the monument. And I kept thinking that I should be shopping for a dress for her. And I thought how during the last two years I had been ill and did not have the strength to shop for a dress. Her *Bat Mitzvah* was in May and I had had the brain operation at the very end of February. A friend offered to go shopping with Chana for a dress for the *Bat Mitzvah*. They bought a lovely suit. They had a good time. In fact I think Barbara had more patience than I would have had under the best of circumstances. I do not think that my Chana minded. Did you, my darling child? And here we were shopping for a tombstone. The owner's name was Mr. Rosenberg and he was very kind. There were three types of stone. The nicest was marble from Italy. Yisrael thought that maybe we should get that. It was as if this was the last thing we would do for our daughter and it must be done well. I did not want stone from outside *Eretz Yisrael*. There were two types of Israeli stone, and we bought the more expensive. And then we had to decide what to write on the stone. It was a week of great tension and I kept thinking that I will not survive. I wanted it to be done by the *sheloshim* (thirty-day mourning period). I was more or less a sounding board but it was Yisrael who composed the text. And he agonized over each word. It had to be beautiful for Chana. What else can he do for her? He used to shop with her, he used to study with her, he used to do everything possible that would make her life a little easier. And now this was the only thing left to do.

I stand on the top of the steps and look at the grave. It is white and shining in the Yerushalayim sun. The black letters stand out. We had the model of a book put on the head of the monument and on the book we had written the phrase from the Book of Ruth which she quoted in her *Bat Mitzvah* speech. "Where you lie, I will lie . . . and there I will be buried." We had the monument made with a slight incline so that when it rains the water will run off. I stand at the top of the steps and look down at the grave. It is white and shining in the Yerushalayim sun. A phrase comes to my lips. "As a rose among the thorns." Am I crazy? Am I talking about the grave? Or does it seem to me that my little girl is lying there with her head on a pillow? So serene and so sweet. The grave and my child are all mixed up in my head. Why do I stay at the top of the steps? I have to see and speak to Chana. And I go down the steps. And I speak to my child.

Thanking the Lord for Affliction?

Aryeh A. Frimer

W E SING IN *HALLEL*, the traditional song of praise and thanksgiving, "I thank You [Lord] *ki anitani* and for being my salvation" (Psalms 118:21). We usually translate *ki anitani* as "for You have *answered* me"; however, *Midrash Tehilim* and several later sources understand *anitani* to stem from the word *inui* or affliction. The verse therefore means: "I thank You [Lord] because You have *afflicted* me and [thereby] have been my salvation." But how are we to understand gratitude for having been afflicted?

Rabbi Abraham Joshua Twerski, the noted psychiatrist and specialist in substance abuse, points out in his Haggadah *From Bondage to Freedom* that it is not easy to attain spiritual growth (which I take to mean the ability to go beyond the demands of the body towards some higher ideal): "It calls for self-sacrifice and for denying oneself many of the things people consider to be the pleasures of life.... People instinctively avoid pain and may avoid spiritual growth because of the discomfort it entails. But an addict has no choice: if he is to recover, he must improve the quality of his spirituality, otherwise he will relapse. This is why recovered addicts may be grateful for their suffering, because it was the only stimulus that could bring them to spirituality." I thank You Lord because Your *affliction* has led to my salvation.

Allow me to suggest a slightly different approach which pivots on the conjunction *ki*, a word with multiple meanings in Hebrew (Talmud, *Rosh Hashanah* 3a). "*Ki*" sometimes means "because" – and this is how R. Twerski understands it. But *ki* can also mean "even though." Both meanings appear in a single verse in Exodus 13:18: "When Pharaoh sent the people out, God did not lead them along the main road that runs through Philistine territory, *even though* [*ki*] that was the shortest route to the Promised Land, *because* [*ki*] God said, 'If the people are faced with a battle, they might change their minds and return to Egypt.'" Hence, I would prefer to interpret this verse as: "I thank You [Lord], *even though* You have afflicted me, for giving me the strength to survive and persevere."

Of course, no one willingly chooses suffering – even if it results in spiritual growth. This is analogous to the Rabbinic dictum (*Midrash Tanhuma, Balak*, sec. 6) about the bee: "Neither of your honey nor your stinger" – we would forego your honey if it means that we could forgo your stinger. Nevertheless, life does not always give us choices. Those who have suffered – and reconstructed their lives in a positive and creative fashion – have acquired a unique strength, a certain credibility that others lack. Indeed, my wife and I lost a child to cancer more than a decade ago. But we made a willed decision not to wallow in our sadness – but go on with the business of life, devoting our energies towards strengthening our family, being creative and communally involved. Having lost a child, I know that I can turn to grieving parents, testify about my loss, and describe my life before and after. I can then tell them that *if they will it*, there is a good productive life after and notwithstanding death. Despite the gaping hole that forever remains, there is much good in life to live for – personal growth, family and community, vocation or avocation.

Sometimes, mourners are skeptical of my message. They cannot hear it because the wound is too fresh, the pain too sharp. But as the days pass, the lesson is slowly internalized – and that is: the struggle to live with the pain of the loss is indeed worth it! Of course, it is not the life I would have chosen. But given that these are the cards I have been dealt, I thank the Creator for the strength to persevere and transmit the positive message to others. It is a gift I dare not squander.

I learned this message from two individuals. One is my wife Esther who would guide us all through our tragedy by coaching us to remain upbeat and not wallow in the justified sadness. "Just put one foot in front of the other," she would say, "and keep moving forward." It helped jump-start our lives and move forward. The second is Rabbi Emanuel Feldman, rabbi emeritus of Congregation Beth Jacob of Atlanta, Georgia. He happened to be in Israel when my son Yaakov *z"l* passed away and, despite the fact that our acquaintance was only casual, he troubled himself to come to be *menahem avel*. This prolific writer and respected Jewish leader had suffered a similar loss of a child and wanted to strengthen us with the knowledge that there was much to live for. His visit made a strong impression on me. There can be much life after death.

I reject those who counsel moving forward because "what other choice is there?" On the contrary, there are always choices (be they depression, suicide, insanity) even if they are tragic themselves. The decision of "*u-vaharta ba-hayyim,* choose life" (Deut. 30:19) is a true act of *gevurah* (bravery) and should be appreciated as nothing less.

I would like to share with the reader a story I heard from Rabbi Shlomo Riskin of Efrat regarding the Klausenburger Rebbe, Rabbi Yekutiel Yehudah Halberstam. Rabbi Halberstam lost his wife and eleven children in the Holocaust. Upon arrival to the United States in 1947, he began rebuilding his family and a large community around him. A decade later, he established the Kiryat Sanz neighborhood in the city of Netanya, Israel. In 1968 he founded yet another Sanz community in Union City, New Jersey. He was also responsible for the construction of Laniado Hospital in 1974 in Netanya. A true builder of Israel!

Shortly after he arrived in New York, the Klausenburger Rebbe was asked to speak at a *brit*. The Klausenburger Rebbe commented on the verse from the Prophet Ezekiel (16:6): "And I saw you wallowing in your blood and I said to you, *be-damayikh hayi.*" This is normally translated as: 'in your blood live!' However, said the Klausenburger Rebbe, the word *be-damayikh* perhaps stems from the word "silence" as in (Lev. 10:3) "*va-yiddom Aharon,* and Aharon was silent [upon hearing of the death of his son's Nadav and Avihu]."

Continued the Klausenburger Rebbe, if our response to tragedy and pain is to wallow in crying, then we Jews who have much to cry about are justified in engaging in endless crying. But then we would not have the energy for anything else. Our grief would consume us! We would not rebuild our lives. We would not rebuild our families; we would not rebuild our institutions; we would not rebuild our future. So like Aaron, we Jews individually and communally choose to limit our mourning – and focus our energy by meeting adversity and tragedy with faith, determination and creative productive action.

Rabbi Joseph B. Soloveitchik (in *Reflections of the Rav,* by R. Abraham Besdin) has noted that in the beginning of creation, God was surrounded by darkness, and the Lord declared: "Let there be light." The verse (Deut. 28:9) "Walk in His ways" bids us to imitate God – *imitatio Dei.* Hence, says the Rav, in our personal lives, when we too are faced by tragedy and surrounded by darkness, the Jewish response is to say: "Let there be light!" – to restart the creative process by rebuilding and reconstructing.

But, it is also important to recognize that the experience of suffering also sensitizes us to the needs of others – an important character building experience. Indeed, that has been true for us on the national as well as the personal level. As Rabbi Soloveitchik points out in his book *Abraham's Journey*,

> "... the central experience in Abraham's life was *galut*—homelessness, wandering without knowing the destination, sleeping on the ground on freezing cold nights, being lost along the byways of a strange land. This passional experience taught Abraham and his descendants the art of involvement, of sharing in distress, of feeling for the stranger, of having compassion for the other. It trained Abraham to react quickly to suffering, to try to lighten the other's burden as much as possible. No matter who the stranger was, what he stood for, and how primitive he was, the stranger had suffered, and suffering purges a person and redeems him ....
>
> Our nation was born in the crucible of exile, bondage, and suffering. We emerged as a people from the sand dunes of the Sinai Desert, where we wandered forty years. . . . If our morality had to be one of kindness and *hesed*, it could not have been formulated for people who knew not what suffering is. Only people in exile could understand and appreciate a morality of kindness. Therefore, *galut* was a central experience in the life of our patriarchs and it is still a major experience in our lives." *

I'm sure that each of us has asked themselves: Why did *Hashem* deem it necessary to send us down to Egypt to be enslaved and suffer? Perhaps, He felt that there were national lessons to be learned that could not be imparted any other way. Many of the lessons of life are experiential. Indeed, the Egypt experience is the underlying rationale for more than fifty *mitzvot* and observances. Every Seder Night we are obligated to re-experience the bitterness of the bondage and the exhilaration of the freedom.

---

* Rabbi Joseph B. Soloveitchik, *Abraham's Journey: Reflections on the Life of the Founding Patriarch* (Jersey City, NJ: Toras HoRav Foundation & Ktav, 2008), pp. 196–197.

Every year we are required to become re-sensitized to the suffering of the downtrodden by eating *maror*.

Should Jews be thankful for suffering in the Egyptian exile? I think not. But should we be thankful for what we learned from it and for the type of nation we have become? Most definitely! Should I be thankful for the death of my beloved son? Of course not! But am I thankful for the insights it has given me, for the power it invested in me to help others and bring them some guidance and comfort? Unquestionably! I thank You Lord, even though You have afflicted me, for giving me the strength to survive and persevere.

Celebrating the Soul

Bernie Kastner

WHEN OUR 19-YEAR-OLD SON Gedalia z"l passed away, we searched for a way to understand what had happened. The more we read about the journey of a Jewish *neshamah*, a precious soul, the more we became strengthened. In effect we discovered self-help in the form of bibliotherapy – simply, healing through the reading of books. Indeed, my first suggestion to parents who lost a child is bibliotherapeutic intervention. Through our readings we learned that we were not alone in encountering such pain; we were encouraged to talk about our loss, plan a constructive course of action and relieve emotional or mental pressure. We saw that there is more than one solution to a problem, gained an understanding of human behavior or motivations, and undertook an honest self-appraisal. Most importantly for us, when we opened our eyes to what may lie in the world beyond, it gives us a glimmer of hope that perhaps one day we will be united with our beloved departed one.

I imagine a great debate that once raged in heaven. It was over a most beautiful and precious new soul that God had created. The angels debated what should be done with this soul. One group of angels demanded that this soul remain in heaven. "She is too pure, too holy to face the ugliness of the lowly world," they said. "Who knows what will happen to her in a world of temptation and evil. This soul must stay with us here." But the other group of angels said the exact opposite: "Indeed this soul glows with a unique divine glow. But for that very reason she must go down to earth. For imagine the beauty and goodness this soul can bring to a dark world. What good is there in keeping such a soul in heaven? Let her descend to earth and shine her light there."

And so they argued back and forth, each side unshakable in their view.

Until it became clear that they could not resolve the issue themselves, they needed a Higher Authority. The case was brought before God Almighty. The angels stated their arguments before the heavenly court. God listened to the two opinions – the first group of angels arguing that this unspoiled soul is too holy to be plunged into the lowly world, the second countering that the world needs such souls more than anything.

And this, I imagine, was God's response: "Indeed, it is sad to send such an immaculate soul into such a dark world. But this is My will. I only created darkness so souls like this one can transform darkness into light. The whole purpose of creation was that the lowly world be refined by the good deeds of mortal human beings. This cannot be achieved by souls in heaven. It can only be achieved through souls in bodies. And so even this most perfect and pure soul must descend to earth."

The first group of angels – who requested for the soul to remain in heaven – was disappointed. They couldn't fathom how such a spiritual being could be expected to survive such a physical world. God turned to them and said, "As for your request to keep this soul up here, I will grant it partially. Though she must leave us and go down to earth, it will not be long before she will return to us. Her sojourn on earth will be brief. Such a brilliant soul will not need long to fulfill her mission. Soon she will be free to come back to heaven."

God then turned to the second group and asked, "Are you satisfied with that? Do you accept that this soul can only be on earth for a limited time?" The angels replied, I am sure, "Yes we do. Every day that she is on earth is a blessing."

When a loved one passes away, we feel we have lost something precious. We are left with a gaping hole in our hearts, and we wonder why they were taken away from us. But at the same time, we can be grateful for the very fact that they were given to us in the first place. We were blessed to have such beautiful souls in our lives. The world is privileged to have such heavenly guests come down on earth. And even if it can only be for a short while, we will take whatever we can get.

I must admit that I find it difficult to imagine coping with a loss without a basic Jewish perspective of the afterlife. A sense of comfort and a healthy dose of inspiration highlight the advantages that this perspective has given to the many grieving parents. But what do we really know about what is out there waiting for us or what took place before we arrived on the scene? How would that knowledge affect our lives today?

I found that our sources are filled with direct and indirect references to surviving after death. Terms such as "going" and "coming," "gathering" and "leaving," are commonly used to allude to the afterlife (see Job 16:22 and 5:26, Ecclesiastes 1:4 and 1:5, Genesis 15:15, Jeremiah 51:39, Deuteronomy 31:16, I Kings 2:7). "And he was gathered unto his people" (Genesis 49:33) is a reference to the deceased being greeted by friends and relatives when he gets to the end of the tunnel and into the bright light of *olam habba*.

Likewise, I found that similar references abound in the Zohar and in the Talmud. Two such references (*Pesahim* 50a, *Bava Batra* 10b) tell us of Rav Yosef the son of Rav Yehoshua ben Levi, who fell ill and died, and then (according to Rashi) came back to life shortly thereafter. This is the first case that we know of in all of Jewish literature of someone undergoing a near-death experience. When his father asked him what he saw, he said "an upside-down world." Those who were considered in this world to be respected and rich were lowly there, and those who were lowly here were on the highest spiritual level there. Whereupon his father responded: "You saw clearly indeed." In *Rosh Hashanah* 17a, Rav Huna, son of Rav Yehoshua, told Rav Papa of his dying and then coming back to life. Rav Papa then said to him: because you always treated others by giving them the benefit of the doubt, here too you were judged according to the exact letter of the law, and hence you were given latitude in meriting more years of life in this world. In *Bemidbar Rabbah* 14 it says that when we were standing as a nation at *Har Sinai* to receive the Torah, all those present died after hearing the first commandment directly from God. The Talmud (*Shabbat* 88) quotes Rav Yehoshua ben Levi who said: after every commandment was given at Mount Sinai, the souls of the Jewish nation departed to the next world. If this is the case, then after the first commandment when everyone died, how did the nation receive the rest of the commandments? The Talmud answers that *Hashem* covered the nation in a special dew that is destined to be used in the World to Come when all the dead will rise once again. This dew was used then to revive each and every one of those who stood at Mt. Sinai.

We need to allow ourselves to be happy when a new child is born and be saddened upon a death. A newborn is full of hope and innocence – a bundle of joy. A death leaves us empty-handed yearning for the departed's presence. Nonetheless, we should recognize that once the proscribed mourning period is over, we should not overdo it. We ought not to stay stuck in our bereavement. We need to move forward by recognizing the wonderful lessons the departed left behind for us to emulate. This would be the appropriate time to understand that their soul is moving on to spiritual heights and true comfort in the next world. It would also be a time to celebrate the soul's courage – having weathered the storm here on earth, no matter how short, and to remember him or her for generations to come.

A Lifetime Later:
Reflections of a Child and Son

Shalom Carmy

I WAS FIVE YEARS OLD and aware of the reason for the pre-dawn ambulance and my mother's abrupt, blood-stained departure. At first there was hope for my brother's survival: hence it was several days before my initial joy surrendered to knowledge of the outcome.

Though the theory that children believe in the omnipotence of wishes has always seemed plausible to me, I cannot remember a time when I was subject to that illusion myself. Nonetheless I took the loss hard. To be joined by a younger brother was the most cherished dream of my childhood. I had not yet studied the *halakhah* according to which misfortune engenders an obligation to engage in self-examination, but a less sophisticated formulation of this principle vividly recommended itself to my consciousness and conscience, and I meditated deeply on those deficiencies of character that may have made me unworthy of the privileges and responsibilities which I associated with having a brother. If the psychologists ever get their claws into me, and suggest that my choice of teaching as a vocation, and the manner in which I have personalized my work, express a desire to compensate for this early experience of inadequacy, I would not be inclined to disagree. (Regretfully, I don't recall being very concerned about my parents' grief.)

The terminology of death did not, as far as I can recollect, provoke a crisis in this budding philosopher. Yet it seems inevitable that young children will be confused by the notion, and not only because "going to heaven" is geographically vague, and phrases like "we lost the baby"

The first section of this essay originally appeared in Yamin and Dvorah Levy, *Confronting the Loss of a Baby: A Personal and Jewish Perspective* (Jersey City, NJ: Ktav Publishing House, 1998).

insinuate an unpardonable degree of absent-mindedness. Closer to home, a child who learns about death will naturally be anxious about the possibility that he or she or the parents may die too. How this is handled will depend on whether death is presented as something bad, which is the view of *halakhah*, or as something good, as is often maintained by more otherworldly religious traditions. If death is good, then it's a wonder that one's parents would care to stick around. If it is bad, then why does it happen?

The most obvious religious explanation is that "God took the baby (or grandfather, etc.); God determined that they weren't needed anymore and God knows best." I'm not sure that this formula is completely satisfactory. To begin with, one wonders how this idea meshes with other information the child has about God. The death-preoccupied child can end up thinking of God exclusively or primarily in the role of Grim Reaper lurking in the shadows, always liable to snatch another loved one, in His infinite wisdom, to eternal bliss. At a practical level, the appeal to God's will does not resolve the child's anxiety about the immediate future.

In a recent conversation with a close friend who was mourning a stillbirth and recounting his two-year old son's reactions, I suggested that it might be safer, and more realistic, to tell the child that people ordinarily don't die until they are ready for death and that such readiness does not come until the person has lived a great deal and accomplished their work in life. The idea of "being ready," or "not yet ready," to do something, is already available to the child in everyday life. It conveys a sense of ripeness and timeliness to one's death that is absent when it is regarded as the inscrutable decree of a distant deity. This presentation enables parents to explain that neither they, nor the child, are likely to die soon, and fits the "normal" experience of dying people whom the child is likely to encounter, who are in one way or another, given the opportunity to become reconciled to their imminent demise. (The risk in this explanation, of course, is that it is susceptible to falsification: a favorite relative or friend could be run over by a car, and it is difficult to sustain the insight that such tragedies are timely and round out full lives.)

*

My mother knew that Yamin and Dvorah Levy had lost a baby. She was presented a copy of Yamin's book on their loss when it came out. She was then in her late 80's. Given the deterioration of her eyesight by then I doubt that she would have read the book through unprompted and located the passage in which she is mentioned. I did not bring it to her attention, as she never alluded to the babies she had lost.

My mother was the youngest of eight children. She was always pleased to have grown up in a large family. A ninth died in childhood and my mother bore her name Hayya. Of her surviving siblings, four were murdered during or after World War II. She married a few years after the war, already in her late thirties. This did not strike me as unusual since many in our circle were starting to have families late in life, sometimes for the second time.

During her first pregnancy my mother was already suffering from the fibroid tumors that interfered with the survival of her children and eventually led to a hysterectomy. Midway through that pregnancy she required surgery for appendicitis. Abortion was illegal, to say nothing of the religious prohibition, yet the doctor, considering how much pain I was causing her, asked my father if he would mind very much if the pregnancy ended as a byproduct of the surgery.

My father was no feminist, but the pain in question was his wife's, not his, and so he told the doctor it was her decision, not his. The doctor opened the conversation by asking Mrs. Carmy how many children she hoped to raise. The middle-aged patient answered six. The doctor gave up on further discussion. The pregnancy continued to term (actually a bit beyond the due date) and its product is writing these words a lifetime later.

At the age of eight, I was assigned the task of writing a short autobiography. I recall being pre-med at the time and also trying to say nice things about the school I was attending. A couple of years ago, long after *Confronting the Loss of a Baby: A Personal and Jewish Perspective* appeared, I found this essay. The flattery was not quite as phony as I had thought. The real surprise, however, was that in this wary, compulsory third-grade exercise in self-revelation I had confessed my deep regret that my parents did not have other children. The composition came into my possession because my mother kept it among her papers for almost fifty years, through all the moves and vicissitudes of her later life.

As I said, my mother never spoke about her failure to reenact the large family she had enjoyed as a child. (After the hysterectomy there was some talk of adoption, but my father was almost seventy and my mother not young and it came to nothing.) On one occasion, late in her life, I was present when she brought her experience to bear.

It was a few years after the book appeared. My mother could still walk unaided, and she strove to maintain her independence. Yet this evening she could not manage alone. Upon my return home she told me something had happened; she had been thinking about it all day; she could not face it alone and wanted me to accompany her immediately so that she could do what must be done. What had happened is the death of an infant in the neighborhood.

The *shivah* was segregated. From the male side of the room I could not hear every word my mother said to the bereaved mother. She, who was by nature the very opposite of an intrusive person, took the floor and spoke as if she had prepared a speech, which is apparently what she had done.

Her message was simple, though it took a few minutes for her to deliver it emphatically. You must not allow what you have suffered to compromise or undermine your devotion to your other children. It is possible that at some point she looked the other in the eye and told her, in a low voice, that she spoke from experience. If she did so, I missed it. What was unmistakable is that she spoke with a knowingness and intensity and authority. Her message was not *about* her experience though it emanated *from* her experience.

Having said what she wanted to say, my mother was silent. After a few minutes she signaled to me that her task had been performed and it was time to go.

At one level, my mother's performance went against the conventional norms according to which we should allow the mourner to control the conversation. On second thought, she did not come to the house of mourning for conversation: she had no personal reminiscences of the deceased infant; she had no interest in passing the time with a young woman she hardly knew; and she certainly took no pleasure in uttering theological bromides or recounting pious anecdotes. She believed that she had something valuable to communicate and that this might contribute to the welfare of the mourner and her family.

I don't know whether the young mother appreciated the words of her elderly neighbor. Our best intentions often fall short of the mark. Yet it was impossible to witness this scene without recognizing that my mother took the mourner's situation with the utmost seriousness. She did not commit the crime, so frequent when we are called upon to comfort those we do not know well, or when we do understand the human condition very well, of treating suffering trivially. If we have lived long enough we have all collected examples of insensitive remarks in difficult moments: opining that children do not suffer much because their bodies are small or that it is good to hear that the child's suffering was prolonged for several years because it gave her parents time to get ready for her death. The beginning of wisdom is to treat suffering seriously.

As noted, my mother took the visit seriously enough to prepare for it. She chose her words deliberately and carefully. She understood that if the human experience of suffering is a serious matter, so is the language with which we address it. She did not treat language, in such situations, as chatter, as a way to fill time. My mother was not an omnivorous reader, but the fiction she valued—Camus, Chekhov, Greene, Tolstoy, Unamuno—she reflected on, and it reinforced the ethical conviction that what is worth saying is worth saying accurately and carefully. If she had read Robert Frost's "Home Burial," a magnificent poem that dramatizes the misunderstandings and alienation that can destroy a couple in the aftermath of a child's death, she would have appreciated and applied its insight. Perhaps nowhere more than in the house of mourning is the absence felt of the kind of psychological sensitivity and disciplined language that we should be getting from great literature.

Notice that my mother avoided another deadly bromide of consolation, one that superficially resembles the approach she took. She did not tell her grieving neighbor to take comfort in her other children, or in the hope that she would have other "replacement" children. Such statements are religiously objectionable, because they presuppose that children are fungible, and that one may replace them as one replaces a worn-out object. Moreover, it is not at all obvious that the mourner shares this debased vision of childbearing, and thus risks giving offense. Instead of speculating without evidence about God's plans or about the needs and desires of her neighbor, my mother concentrated on her categorical responsibilities—to care for her living children.

This move, too, is not without risk. At that moment the grieving woman might not be ready to think of her real ongoing duties and might resent the reminder. But it is better, I think, to err on the side of reality, which ultimately cannot be denied, than to engage in the wild fantasy and idle sentimentality that we often mistake for the exhibition of piety. Sooner or later the claims of her children will assert themselves, and it is better to have been alerted beforehand to the importance of not neglecting these responsibilities than to drift into neglect or obliviousness, which harden into habit, at which point the gentle voice of responsibility is transmuted into the grating rasp of rebuke, and before patterns take hold that cannot be easily or painlessly undone.

In the end, of course, no serious human intercourse is without risk and vulnerability. The best we can do, as *immi morati* sought to do over her long life, is to meet our responsibilities in fear and trembling and resoluteness.

Yellow Fire Trucks

David Fine

YELLOW FIRE TRUCKS!? ALL the stories my mom had read to me had pictures of red fire trucks. Fire trucks were supposed to be red not yellow! And why were these yellow fire trucks coming to my Bobe's and Aunt Annie's house on *Pesach*? I didn't understand what was happening then at the tender age of three but I knew one thing – that whatever was happening, it wasn't good. We were all outside on my Bobe's large veranda and my mother was wailing and screaming. She was hugging people, some of whom I recognized and some who were complete strangers. To this day I am not sure whether my mom knew them either. Jeremy, my three-month-old brother, had died of Sudden Infant Death Syndrome (SIDS). I was suddenly not a big brother anymore. Actually, I was not any brother. It would be more than two years until I would become a big brother again.

These few moments on my grandmother's veranda, my mother crying, the yellow fire trucks – these are the only memory I have of the entire episode. It is also my earliest memory, the very first thing that I remember. This episode is eternally seared on my memory. I may not see it for months but ultimately it returns. It drops in and lingers for a moment or two and then disappears just as quickly. It is a constant reminder that life can be snuffed out in a second, a constant reminder of what could have been. A constant reminder of the ultimate question: why?

Almost ten years later I had my *Bar Mitzvah*. I read the portion of *Ki Tetze* which includes the verse in Deuteronomy 24:16: "The fathers shall not be put to death for the children, neither shall the children be put to death for the fathers: every man shall be put to death for his own sin." Everywhere I turned I saw a reminder of Jeremy. What sin did he commit? I was still too young to understand that I would never understand.

My life has become one of questioning that led me to enhanced religious observance and a life in the rabbinate. Life is funny sometimes. Here I was, a person who was somewhat angry at God and often questioned Him and I was becoming a rabbi!

We all deal with these things differently. I, myself, never told any of my friends about Jeremy until I was older. Now I talk about it often and sometimes even with my own children. But not with my parents. Why? Should I? More wonder – always more wonder. Would my younger brother Adam have been my brother had Jeremy not died? Would he have been the best man at my wedding or would it have been Jeremy? Was my parents' plan to have two kids or three? Was one brother supposed to replace the other? Is this what Adam thought? If he did, I wonder how it made him feel.

Over time, Jeremy has become my companion throughout life even though he is not physically there. While at times this made me sad and mad as it made me wonder how much better things would have been – Bobe should have brought all three of us – me, Jeremy and Adam – to Centre Island and Ontario place. When Adam and I and my cousins stole the sign that said we shouldn't walk on the grass from my Nana's condominium Jeremy should have been there. It would have made it even more fun – it has also allowed me to celebrate life's joys with him. This has helped me focus on the blessing in my life. This has helped me become a more grateful person. Jeremy is still an everlasting presence in my life as I feel him at times peering over my shoulder.

Sometime after my Bobe's funeral in 1997, I read Rabbi Joseph B. Soloveitchik's *Kol Dodi Dofek* in which he discusses the issue of evil in the world and why righteous people suffer. When humans don't find answers they get frustrated and there are no answers that would satisfy the human psyche when it comes to these lofty questions. The questions that one must ask, according to Rabbi Soloveitchik, are not the questions of "why" – because those we will never understand – but rather the questions of "what." What can I do as a result of this tragedy that will make me a better person and that can help me make the world a better place? My experiences made me feel as if he was talking directly to me. It has been a manifesto for me as I have counseled many a family dealing with tragedy. While people can never really stop speculating about the "why," by focusing on the "what" they are able to put the tragedy that they have experienced to some productive use through their contributions that they make. As a result they memorialize the deceased which ultimately eases their pain in some small way.

To focus on the "what" instead of the "why" is one of life's biggest challenges. By nature, human beings like answers not questions. We despise uncertainty. It's uncomfortable. We like to make sense of the world. I often wonder – would Jeremy have been a fan of the Mets or Yankees? Would he have liked chocolate ice cream or vanilla? Would he have been an Aristotelian or a Neo-Platonist? Would he too have become a rabbi? A lawyer? A doctor? Would he have liked Shlomo Carlebach? The Grateful Dead? Avraham Fried? These questions often make me sad and angry at God. These are emotional reactions which do not respond well to intellectual solutions.

I have been taught by my parents, by my tradition, by my community and most important by my wife to always try to find the good in everything, to locate the silver lining. Easier said than done. Sometimes, I at least try not to succumb to the Grateful Dead's feeling that "every silver lining has a touch of grey." Can there be a silver lining to the death of a three-month-old baby? The question itself is almost ludicrous. But there must be something. The answer has become clear to me and this I do not wonder about. My grappling with this challenge throughout my life has made me a better rabbi and a better counselor. While studying about counseling and pastoral psychology in rabbinical school is helpful – one becomes a good counselor by being one. When you experience tragedy, death, wonder, questions, anger and the inexplicable you become better equipped to help others struggle with these things.

Rabbi Soloveitchik also has a well-known teaching about mourning and the difference between personal mourning and national mourning, specifically as it relates to *Tisha Be-Av*. We do not mourn the same way for these two experiences. National mourning for the Temple and other communal tragedies is more difficult. He terms this "*Avelut Yeshanah*." We never witnessed the Temple standing in its glory. We did not experience its splendor, its beauty and sublimity. How can we mourn something that we never knew? It is much more difficult than mourning a loved one whom we loved and cherished and experienced life with so the mourning process must differ. When a loved one dies it is sadder and easier to mourn. We knew them. We lived with them and we know exactly what we are missing. The *halakhot* as they apply to these two types of *avelut* are different. While chronologically Jeremy's death was contemporary, my *avelut* for Jeremy is *Avelut Yeshanah*. It happened a long time ago. I didn't know him and while I can imagine his presence I don't really know what I am missing.

My parents have really never spoken with me in any great detail about their thoughts, their feelings about losing a child. I was always too scared to initiate the conversation out of fear that talking about it would hurt them. As I write this essay I understand that I have never really processed this tragedy either. How could I expect others to process what I never have? In rabbinical training we are taught to talk to people, to draw out their thoughts, to help them process. While this may be healthier, sometimes we have to respect the wishes of people not to talk. Knowing when to do this is a real challenge.

When my first son was born I asked my parents whether I should name him Jeremy. My mother did not think it was a good idea. I listened. It was the right decision. No wondering about this one.

One of my favorite songs is "Forever Young" by Rod Stewart. It is about a parent who does not want his child to ever grow up. Sometimes I drive in my car and listen to this song over and over and I cry. I cry because Jeremy is forever young. He did not have the life that he should have had.

Should I have felt guilty my whole life that it was him that died and not me? I have never thought about this on a conscious level and I have never actively felt guilty. I have had a blessed life. God has given me all I could ever want. I see that I have found something new to wonder about. But wondering is good. Rabbi Abraham Joshua Heschel said that "wonder is the root of all knowledge." Would Jeremy have read Heschel?

I read my kids stories like many parents do. Many of them are about fire trucks and firemen. None of the fire trucks have ever been yellow. I wonder why.

The Knowledge of Pain

Avraham (Avie) Walfish

HALLELI

S OMETHING ABOUT THE PLIGHT of one-and-a-half year old Halleli, struggling for her life in the Pediatric Intensive Care Unit (PICU) of Shaare Zedek Medical Center in Jerusalem, captured the public imagination even beyond the normal fascination we humans experience upon encountering tragedy. Undoubtedly my granddaughter Halleli's age and the horrifically freaky nature of her accident played a role in stirring empathy, but I don't know the full reason that her mysteriously "photogenic" plight – weeks before her picture appeared in electronic and printed media – evoked such a widespread outpouring of prayers and *mitzvot* on behalf of her recovery. In her brief life Halleli was a highly unusual child, famous among neighboring parents for her easygoing good nature, and as her life drew to a close she continued to elicit the highest and noblest of human responses.

I have replayed in my head so often the scene of Halleli's accident that I feel as though I had been there. The innocent game of hide-and-seek, Halleli's favorite, behind the low-hanging curtain – specially designed for nursery toddlers. Contriving to maneuver her head between the curtain and the wire from which it hung, Halleli swiftly lost consciousness, her legs still visible to her nursery teacher beneath the curtain. Feeding two other tots, occasionally addressing a remark to Halleli, the nursery teacher fails to note her lack of response during those long moments when she might have been saved. The horror of the discovery. The hysterical phone calls to Avia (my daughter-in-law, Halleli's mother), far away in Jerusalem, and to my son Shlomo, poring over his folio of Talmud in the local Tekoa yeshiva. Shlomo's frantic attempts at resuscitation, the arrival of the paramedics, who after agonizingly protracted efforts succeeded in restoring a pulse – but not respiration.

Ultimately, like myriads of other people, my family and I experienced the death of our beloved Halleli and embarked on the long journey of grief and emotional healing. However, the moments I relive endlessly relate not to the finality of death, but to the tricky borderline separating death from life. For several weeks Halleli's condition defied precise definition as alive or dead. Indeed the determination of Halleli's death was brought about ultimately not by any change in her physical condition, but by a change in the way in which her condition was regarded by rabbis and doctors. Following the determination of death a mini-drama ensued, capped by the donation of four of Halleli's organs to four deathly-ill children, bringing us face to face with the paradoxical meeting point between our tragedy and the joy of four other families. I would like to share with you some of the experiences and lessons garnered during these few weeks.

DEATH AS CONDITION OR DEFINITION

For three days, Halleli's condition seesawed between the near collapse and the recovery of liver, kidneys, and other organs, and despite the overwhelming odds we continued to hope that a miracle might, just might, happen. Some of us struggled with a nagging doubt whether we indeed wished for the miracle to occur – we had every reason to fear that if Halleli would miraculously survive, she would be permanently and severely brain-damaged. Dare we hope and pray for the miracle within a miracle that will restore to us Halleli as she was?

On the fourth day, Halleli's weak and sporadic spontaneous respiration ceased entirely, indicating that the brain stem was no longer functioning. As the doctors commenced the battery of clinical tests that would confirm the lack of brain-stem function, the attending pediatric neurologist – Prof. Avraham Steinberg, a distinguished expert in *halakhic* medical ethics – prepared us for the process which would finalize the diagnosis of brain-stem death. Protocol required confirming the clinical results by means of an "instrumental" examination, a Trans-Cranial Doppler (TCD) test which would ascertain that that blood-flow to the brain stem had ceased. No one was more shocked than Prof. Steinberg when Halleli's TCD yielded positive results, indicating continued blood flow to a supposedly dead brain stem. After several repetitions of the TCD over the next few days yielded similar results, Prof. Steinberg explained the complexity of Halleli's condition: "clinically" she was brain-dead, but "definitionally" she was still alive.

Although this was hardly the first time that I had encountered a conflict – always challenging – between scientific reality and *halakhic* norms, there was something particularly unsettling about this one, and not only because of the frayed emotions involved. Intellectually the idea that death was a socially-sanctioned definition rather than a clear-cut biological fact made sense to me. As I reviewed the literature on brain-stem death, I rediscovered what doctors have long known, that certain tissues in the body continue to live and function days after cardiac activity, respiration, and most brain functions have ceased. Short of delaying burial for several days until the body begins to decompose, as certain European countries did in the eighteenth and nineteenth centuries, there is no choice but to select a certain point in the collapse of bodily functions and define it as death. Existentially, however, it is challenging in the extreme to connect the philosophical theory with the concrete presence of a beloved family member whom you know to be biologically "dead," but who continues to "live" – "definitionally."

The paradoxical situation of "not alive but not dead" not only extended our period of anxious limbo for three long weeks, but also confronted us with existential and *halakhic* conundrums with which we continued to grapple. Existentially we struggled with the questions of hope, prayer, and mystical activities. Even before Halleli entered the liminal state between life and death, it was wrenchingly unclear whether one could realistically hope and pray for recovery, or whether we shouldn't reorient hopes and prayers towards – dare one even think it – closure. Following the "clinical" establishment of brain stem death, the rational-realistic answer to this question became painfully clear, but this did not prevent some members of the family, led by Shlomo, from clinging to their faith that the time for miracles had not yet passed. Throughout our three weeks in the hospital, Shlomo amazed me with his ability simultaneously to juggle hard-nosed realism when medical life-and-death decisions were required with a tireless pursuit of kabbalistic remedies designed to engineer a miracle.

Our existential predicament was reflected in occasional *halakhic* enigmas, enabling us to sublimate our battered emotions in the form of

legal dialectic. We wondered, for example, whether we should warn a
kohen friendly with Shlomo who frequented the hospital to stop entering
Halleli's room, occupied as it was by a "clinical" corpse. We decided that
in this matter as well, the "definitional" trumped the "clinical." Ultimately
Halleli "died" not because one organ or another ceased to function, but
because we succeeded in narrowing the gap between clinical and definitional reality. Prodded by the family, Prof. Steinberg, with the approval
of former Chief Rabbi Mordechai Eliyahu, performed a different confir-
matory exam, which, in their determination, enabled them to ignore the
results of the TCD.

The gap between the clinical and the definitional, although ostensibly
closed, reasserted itself one last time after Halleli was officially declared
"dead." Why, Shlomo wondered, should he commence now the process
of *aninut* and *shivah* when Halleli actually had been dead for three weeks?
This question led me to reflect that, no less that death itself, mourning
is a societal phenomenon. The laws and practices of mourning strike a
delicate balance between the mourner's deepest feelings and his social
interactions, and they do not commence until one's private feelings con-
form to the perceptions and expectations sanctioned by the society.

DEATH AS SOURCE OF LIFE

Halleli's liminal state between life and death was a source of anxiety on
more than one level. Keeping Halleli "alive" on machines maintained
the risk that she might continue in this vegetative state indefinitely,
condemning Shlomo, Aviyah, and the rest of the family to an ongoing
relationship with a beloved child who cannot respond or interact in any
way. Most doctors assured us that this would not happen (and I still
shudder to think that for me, my granddaughter's death was the preferred
alternative), but – as one pediatric neurologist told us in a different context – "We doctors are good at explaining what has already happened;
we're much weaker in predicting the future."

There was, however, another, more realistic, fear. When we realized
that Halleli was, in all probability, brain-dead, we began to think of the
possibility that our tragedy might serve as someone else's salvation. Medical protocol prohibits doctors and nurses from broaching with family
members the subject of organ donation until after the official medical
committee has declared the donor to be brain-dead. However, nothing

prevented the family from – gingerly, one by one – raising the issue with the doctors, and discovering that indeed Halleli was a potential donor, and that a potential liver recipient had been located. As long as Halleli's brain-stem death was only "clinical" and not "definitional," the danger grew that Halleli's organs would fail and would be unusable after her death. As we abandoned hope for Halleli's continuing to live, we grew to hope for the more attainable goal that her death might help sustain someone else's life. Ultimately this occurred and our family experienced the tricky boundary line separating life from death from yet another vantage point.

From my experience of the brain-death and organ transplant issue I have drawn important lessons, both practically and experientially. On the practical level, having played a supporting role in determining Halleli's death and donating her organs, I am more firmly committed than ever to accepting irrevocable loss of brainstem function "definitionally" as death. Valuable medical resources should not be expended on maintaining their bodies, and critically ill recipients should be allowed to benefit from their organs.

However, my experience has conditioned me to view the dispute existentially and not only intellectually. Today when I read the *halakhic* literature regarding organ transplantation, I see the flesh-and-blood represented so abstractly in the formalistic categories. When pro-transplant advocates write about the loss of organism integrity upon failure of the brain, I see the inexorable – if unexpectedly slow – loss of Halleli's maintenance of stable blood pressure and later of digestive processes. When anti-transplant advocates write about the signs of life, especially heartbeat, that may continue long after brain-stem death, I see the body of little Halleli, warm and apparently vital, absorbing fluids and nutrition, excreting waste. Having experienced Halleli for three weeks as alive and dead at the same time, I identify with those who wish, as I did, to come to grips with grim reality and move on, while at the same time maintaining sympathy for those, rabbis and family members alike, who cannot accept the notion that a warm functional body may be regarded as dead.

In the aftermath of Halleli's death and donation of her heart, liver, and two kidneys to four deathly-ill children, I was thrust into a mercifully brief career as a media star. In my media appearances, I always tried to emphasize the built-in paradox of organ donations: the same respect for life which militates in favor of utilizing the organs of the dying donor in order to maintain the long-term survival of the recipient also commands us vigilantly to maintain the right to life and the dignity of the donor. Hence, both pro-transplant and anti-transplant positions are ultimately rooted in the same core value of commitment to life and human dignity. The key question is, of course, how we find the proper tradeoff between the life and dignity of the donor and those of the recipient, and here is where the battle lines are drawn. Whether reasonably or unfairly, God has imposed upon mortal humans the responsibility for deciding these complex and emotion-fraught decisions, and I believe that the current medical and legal norms in the State of Israel balance the competing values in optimal fashion.

OF GRANDPARENTING AND PARENTING

One of the first things that I learned in the course of our unfolding tragedy was that every person experiences tragedy differently. As a family learns to confront the harsh reality that has befallen them, they must also learn to accommodate divergent styles and tempos. When one feels like crying, another feels like picking up a guitar and singing. One needs to spend endless time in Halleli's presence, while another can't bear to witness her beloved body with tubes stuffed down her throat. Each family member – parents, grandparents, great-grandparents, uncles and aunts – of necessity has to process his own thoughts and emotions, while at the same time providing support for the rest of the family.

As grandfather I experienced Halleli's injury and ultimate death as a double tragedy: both the loss of a granddaughter and the wrenching grief of a son. The hardest moments for me were the many moments when Shlomo threw himself on Halleli's bed and wept bitterly. All my parental instincts urged me to protect and console, while my intellect cautioned me that I had no protection and no consolation to offer. Useless as I felt on those occasions, I would be called upon to offer parental support at other times and in other ways.

Some of the most difficult moments occurred when Shlomo and Aviyah were called in for medical consultations, usually because of a medical crisis requiring parental decision. How I wished at those moments that the doctors had called me in instead of Shlomo. How could a 24-year-old young man be emotionally equipped to confront such fateful questions about his one and only baby daughter? Did he have the experience and the perspective to decide them wisely? Might an unwise decision condemn him and Aviyah to months, maybe years, of caring for a child in a Permanent Vegetative State (PVS)? Unable to protect my son from the emotional and intellectual challenges of these experiences, I reminded myself that, more than anyone else, it would be Shlomo and Aviyah who would live the rest of their lives with the consequences of their decisions, and no one else could take responsibility for them.

My conviction that Shlomo and Aviyah, whatever their degree of preparation, needed to make their own decisions, was most severely tested at those moments when Shlomo consulted with me or with all the grandparents. Despite the overwhelming parental urge to take charge and to protect, I strove to present my views as ideas for consideration rather than as firm opinions.

Throughout the dark night of our ordeal there were also moments that evoked a different kind of parental emotion, such as se'udah shlishit on our first Shabbat in the hospital, when the family gathered around Halleli's bed for a round of heartfelt zemirot. Amid voices that choked with tears or cracked with sorrow, we sang of a harmonious world and of a God who guides and protects. Grief mingled with devotion, joy with sadness, and I felt the pride of a father whose son navigated the entire family amid the shoals of grief with such presence, such faith, and such love of life.

CONFRONTING GOD IN TRAGEDY

The seudah shlishit experience described above was the first of several such occasions, culminating in the guitar Shlomo produced after Halleli's brain-stem death was officially confirmed, in order to sing to her one last time. Never was God so intensely present for me as during the course of our ordeal, and never was He so inscrutable. Three years after Halleli's tragedy, God blessed Shlomo and Aviyah with twins, a boy and a girl (who resembles Halleli), and their home is filled with life and joy. However, this two-fold replacement of their loss, like the two-fold replacement at the end of the book of Job, provide only partial consolation for the loss, the suffering, and the grief. Job's dramatic story has ended, but his unanswered questions continue to resonate long after we have closed the book. In the wake of my personal drama, there are many things I need to learn about the questions I ask of God and the answers I require. At this stage, I will follow the dictum with which Wittgenstein concluded his first philosophical treatise: Whereof one cannot speak, thereof one must be silent. (This is Wittgenstein's seventh and final "basic proposition" in his *Tractatus Logico-Philosophicus*.)

The Death of the Daughter of Rabbi Hanina

Chaim Licht

Rabbi Hanina's daughter died and he did not cry over her.
His wife said to him, "Is it a chicken you have taken out
of your house?"
He said to her, "Two, bereavement and blindness?"
He thought as Rabbi Yohanan who said in the name
of Rabbi Yossi ben Ketsarta, "There are six kinds of
tears, three are good and three are bad. Of crying and of
smoke and of [stomach pain in the] lavatory are bad, of
laughter and of perfume and of fruit are good."

(SHABBAT 151B-152A, OXFORD MANUSCRIPT 366)

THE MOTHER WHO HAS lost her daughter is distraught because her husband's pain is not visible. He does not show any signs of mourning. Does the death of his daughter not pain him? The reader is dumbfounded by Rabbi Hanina's behavior. Even more so is his wife, who is among those closest to him, if not the closest of all. She looks at his demeanor and not only can she not understand it, but from the way she speaks, it is apparent that it troubles her. Her severe and harsh words assign blame. She makes a sharp and cruel comparison of the daughter to a chicken. Humans raise a chicken in order to enjoy the eggs it lays and eat the meat. By comparing the daughter to a chicken, the woman accuses her husband of not valuing the daughter's life and of accepting her death

This essay is abridged with minor changes from Chaim Licht, *In the Grip of Bereavement: An Analysis of Ten Aggadic Legends on Bereavement in the World of the Sages*, trans. Ronnie Schwartz (Jerusalem: Gefen Publishing House, 2009).

as a desirable outcome. She was destined for slaughter and therefore he is not upset with her death.

She continues with even harsher words, "You have taken out of your house"; that is, he took the daughter out of the house. The simple meaning of the words is that he brought her to burial, but in the analogy to a chicken it appears that the wife is saying to her husband that he took her out to be slaughtered. A great deal of blame is being placed here. Does she blame him for the daughter's death? Does she compare him to the owner of a chicken who brings it to slaughter? Does she blame her husband for lacking any feelings towards the daughter or upon her death? Since the wife used harsh imagery to give full meaning to her words, their implication is clear. The wife's harsh words were said to provoke her husband, the father, from his composure and to cause him to respond with words no less harsh, but surprisingly he remains calm. Apparently, he understands her enormous pain and therefore uses great restraint.

He ignores her harsh words and explains his behavior to her: "Two, bereavement and blindness?" With his words he makes reference to grief and sightlessness. The bereavement is decreed upon him and it hurts him greatly; he has no control over this grief. It was not he who took the daughter out of the house, but God Who brought upon them this tragedy, and it was not in their hands to prevent it. He is not guilty of taking the daughter out to slaughter. By referring to blindness, he apparently means that it is within his power to prevent the blindness and therefore he does not cry. It is not because he does not feel the agony of the daughter's death and not because of indifference to her death, Heaven forbid. He is a bereaved father who is pained by his daughter's death, like every father who lost a daughter, but crying leads to blindness and because of his responsibility, he must prevent bringing another tragedy upon the family. (Our story is related in the Talmud to the description of an old man who loses his physical abilities towards the end of his life. Among others, there is a description of how his tears for his suffering towards the end of his life cause him to become blind. There is no explanation in the story as to how crying brings about blindness.)

From Rabbi Hanina's answer we learn that his wife did not understand his behavior and accused him unjustly. A person who mourns the death of someone dear is not obligated to show his pain; there are those who succeed in controlling and restraining themselves from the relief of pain through tears. And whoever restrains himself does not grieve any less than one who expresses his sorrow in tears. Restraint from crying is not proof of indifference to grief. Rabbi Hanina saw fit to explain to his wife the reason for his not crying, an explanation that teaches that he too wanted to cry as others do, but was prevented because of his responsibility to his family.

The narrator chose not to describe Rabbi Hanina's wife's response to his words but rather to explain to the reader how Rabbi Hanina arrived at his conclusion. It can be assumed that Rabbi Hanina accepted the words of his colleague, Rabbi Yossi ben Ketsarta, and his behavior proves that he tried to put word to deed. According to Rabbi Yossi ben Ketsarta there are tears that cause good to the one who sheds them, as well as the opposite – tears that cause harm to the weeper. Tears are an expression of the emotional state. On one hand, sorrowful crying is a sign of a person's suffering and if he continues crying for an extended period of time, it means that his suffering continues. If he does not overcome it, it is liable to cause him both physical and emotional harm. On the other hand, tears of satisfaction add physical and emotional strength to the one who sheds them. A person who prolongs tears of joy strengthens himself. According to this explanation, Rabbi Hanina conveys to his wife the clear message that he is refraining from crying in order to prevent another tragedy – of blindness – befalling them. If he were to cry he would increase his sorrow by causing emotional and physical damage to the point of blindness.

This is the interpretation given by the narrator in order to link Rabbi Hanina's words and those of Rabbi Yossi ben Ketsarta. I, however, do not think this is Rabbi Hanina's purpose. First, it is hard to understand how a grieving person's crying during the mourning period causes blindness, for the narrator describes the daughter's death and the parents' immediate reactions. The wife's complaint is not made after a protracted and extended period of time following the daughter's death. Second, Rabbi Yossi ben Ketsarta does not mention a specific detriment that is liable to happen to someone who cries during his bereavement. Similarly, he does not mention blindness as a tragedy stemming from crying at all.

It seems to me that it is more accurate to limit the story to Rabbi Hanina's answer to his wife at the end of the first scene. In his answer to his wife's complaint he refers to the bereavement he feels and implies that although it pains him deeply, he is not convinced that tears are a measure of his suffering. Crying is an external expression of internal pain. When a person cries in public, everyone sees his suffering and his pain for the misfortune that befell him. However, this is only an outward expression and contains, therefore, an element of blindness. No one can tell how deep the mourner's pain is according to his tears. It is possible that the crying releases the inner stress and alleviates it for a short time, but there is no release from the great pain for the death of the deceased. In light of this, it seems that the crying causes "blindness" to those around the mourner. It is a sign and indication of mourning.

However, there is a greater possibility that it causes "blindness" to the mourner. When Rabbi Hanina says to his wife that he does not want to go blind, his meaning is that he does not want to minimize his agony over their daughter's death through the release of his tears. He cannot and does not want to hide from the hard questions that weigh upon him. Why did his daughter die? Did she sin? How did she sin? Did she die because of the sins of others? Is it possible to understand her death? It seems to me that Rabbi Hanina says to his wife that bereavement and crying contradict each other. Therefore he says to her, "Two, bereavement and blindness?" His words are full of amazement. Can both exist together? The grief is deep and strong, and crying is liable to lessen the pain and sorrow. Rabbi Hanina does not want this; he does not want to "blind" himself, to lessen the acute pain. Therefore he prevents himself from crying.

Rabbi Hanina's answer creates confusion in understanding the bereaved parents' behavior. The wife asks her husband, "Is it a chicken you have taken out of your house?" It can be concluded that the mother mourns without end. At the same time, her husband's behavior, which arouses the sense that he feels no sorrow for their daughter's death, pains her greatly. Rabbi Hanina's answer indicates that he grieves no less and perhaps even more than his wife; but his way of expressing grief is unlike the accustomed manner and different in style from what his wife expects. The wife views bereavement by external indications, but his style is deep internal grief accompanied by difficult questions, a grief turned inward without any external displays. Everyone mourns in his own way and the style of one should not be forced upon the other. The different ways that the wife and her husband the sage, the bereaved mother and father, express their suffering cannot be used to determine the level of their sorrow and grief, nor whether there is understanding or defiance of God's judgment. The difficult questions about their daughter's death still remain.

According to the narrator, each person has the right to grieve in his own way, and the manner in which he grieves does not indicate how the mourner feels about the reason for the death, nor does it explain the daughter's death or God's decree of her death. The questions remain unanswered because the narrator believes they have no answer. Also, the questions of what will bring comfort to the bereaved parents – crying? silence? – have no answers.

The mother mourning the loss of her daughter expresses her acute pain with tears, which she believes conveys the depth of her anguish and sorrow. This external expression seen by all is a common and reasonable manifestation, because people usually judge others by what they observe; when a person sees the severity of the mourner's outward expression, he views it as testimony to the intensity of the inner pain. Rabbi Hanina's wife represents this belief, and therefore she is angry with her husband who does not cry. In contrast to her, Rabbi Hanina represents the opposite view. He believes that someone whose inner pain is so acute is not capable of crying. Additionally, tears are only an external outlet, a temporary relief of the pain.

The unique concept in Rabbi Hanina's approach to the mourner is to view crying as blindness. It is an illusion of relief from the pain and the grief on one hand; and on the other, it is a false impression of the measure of the intense agony. He is not capable of crying, not capable of being comforted as long as he does not find an answer to his difficult and agonizing questions concerning his daughter's death. He does not cry because he is not able to free himself, not even briefly, from his great sorrow. To him, crying shows the mourner's ability to receive consolation, to become encouraged and overcome his pain; and if he does not cry, he is not able to receive consolation for the daughter's death. The narrator, who added an explanation to Rabbi Hanina's words to his wife, understood his words differently, as an explanation of self-control and restraint that prevents another misfortune of physical blindness, a tragedy that will strike hard not only at him but also at his wife. Therefore, as a sage knowledgeable in the words of another sage, he learned that it is his responsibility to control his tears in order to prevent another misfortune, blindness.

According to this approach, the wife is correct in her view that crying is an accurate expression of the strength of the pain and grief; but it should not persist for a long time because in addition to crying it is liable to cause blindness. The analysis of the story teaches that the explanation is faulty at its foundation, and in my opinion, it is a contrived addition that seems excessive and not apropos. The reader will judge between the two positions and decide according to his understanding whether indeed Rabbi Hanina's intent in the word "blindness" is physical blindness, or the blindness of man in grasping the implications in the world, in our case, of grief.

Marital Challenges Following the Loss of a Child

Miriam Benhaim

THE TORAH, AS A book of life, teaches about human experience in its fullness. The first *mitzvah* given to Adam and Eve, "And God blessed them . . . be fruitful and multiply" (Genesis 1:28), directs our hearts and minds to the future and visions of bounty, blessing and happiness that children bring to the world. The possibility of the death of a child is far from our mindset of hope and positive anticipation when we read this verse. The sad truth however is children die untimely deaths. The parents of the deceased child are forced to set off on an unplanned journey to create meaning in a world in which unimaginable tragedy has occurred.

The loss of a child is a horrific event that can shake the very foundation of our assumptive worlds. Ronnie Janoff-Bulman writes that such an event challenges belief in a benevolent world, belief in an orderly universe, and belief in the worth of the individual. The loss of a child is the seminal example of a traumatic event. It violates the natural order of life and potentially leaves the parent feeling unsafe and vulnerable in what appears to be a random and chaotic world devoid of meaning. At times one's psychological survival may feel threatened as comforting, basic, life-long assumptions about the world and self are upended, particularly the parental role as a protector of one's child.

PARADIGMS OF LOSS

The Torah offers a variety of paradigms and examples of how individuals cope with the loss of a child. Adam and Eve are the first couple to suffer the death of a child when their son Cain kills his brother Abel. We hear nothing from either of them about their reactions to the death of their son. We learn later that they have another son Shet (Seth). Perhaps their silence teaches about a deep sense of shock and mystery in response to the loss of their child. Later in the Torah in the book of Leviticus, following the death of his sons Nadav and Avihu, Aaron is portrayed as actively choosing the stance of silence or the state of being frozen. The word used is *"va-yiddom"* (Leviticus 10:3) which implies that Aaron actively caused himself to be silent. Did he emote first and then become silent? Perhaps his silence helps us to get in touch with deep, unimaginable pain that results from the utter incomprehensibility that often ensues after the loss of an offspring that words can not describe?

King David suffered many losses. Two of his children died and in each case he reacted very differently. In the first story (II Samuel 12: 15–21) he fasted and prayed, prostrated himself on the ground, and begged *Hashem* to spare the child. When he became aware of the fact that the child had died he got up and ate. In the second story (II Samuel 18:33), upon hearing that Absalom had died, David cried out, "Absalom, my son my son who will allow me to die in your stead. / *Avshalom, binee, binee, mi yitten ani muti tahtekha.*" He was beside himself and willing to offer up his life in lieu of his child's. I mention these two different ways of coping with grief by the very same person to highlight how context and circumstances might influence a person's grief response. Consequently, couples, who are two individuals with different histories and psychological makeup, face an enormous challenge navigating the loss of a child together.

These different stories underscore the proposition that there is not just one correct path to deal with the loss of a child. There is a bias in Western culture that the mourner must experience strong affect in order to deal with and work through his or her grief. But the expectation that there is a "right and correct" way to grieve, namely one characterized by free flowing affect and copious expression of sadness, anger and tears, is a very narrow way of approaching the grief process. There are different and valid grief styles to be found within individuals, couples and families, and these differences need to be understood and respected as true expressions of grief over a core level loss.

Terry Martin and Ken Doka divide grieving into two broad patterns. The first is labeled the "intuitive" style, and this closely mimics the traditional Western style in which the individual experiences, expresses, and adapts to loss affectively. The intuitive griever needs opportunities to express emotion and requires a "holding environment" that validates the legitimacy of the emotions being expressed. The second style is characterized as "instrumental," and this expression and adaptation to loss is manifested by cognitive and physical reactions. The instrumental griever sees loss as a problem to be managed or solved, and has a reduced need to express emotion.

When parents are out of synch, coping differently, or at different phases of the grief process, there is potential for enormous strife and discord. There are a plethora of factors that inform our individual coping styles in different situations and each couple is comprised of two complicated people who now must face an unfathomable situation together. It is to be expected that each day will bring with it new demands that will require tremendous understanding of each one's perspective and style of coping, and this can place enormous strain on the relationship. The current literature does not support the old notion that couples confronted with the loss of a child have a much higher rate of divorce. However, it is certainly a time when unresolved and troublesome issues are potentially exacerbated and might create difficulties in even the best relationship. Without recognizing that individuals cope and respond differently to loss, it is easy to see how tension, misunderstanding, enormous disappointment and a decrease in marital intimacy can arise if disparate styles are not validated as legitimate. Of course, these styles cross gender lines, and men and women manifest both styles. It is also true that the lines demarcating these styles are not rigid. Individuals show a bias or strong tendency toward one style or another, yet this does not block the possibility of "mixed" expressions of grief.

By way of example, I worked with a couple who came for treatment soon after the loss of their two month old daughter. The wife, Tzippi, spent many hours sobbing uncontrollably and lamenting that "a hole was cut into my heart." She was furious with her husband, Moshe, and accused him of not caring about the tragedy because he talked about forming a charitable foundation that would pay students to study Torah in memory of their deceased child. While Tzippi valued this project, she experienced Moshe as detached and cold. She could not understand why Moshe did not express or share her feelings of loss and consequently she felt alone and isolated from her husband. Moshe had a myriad of reactions. He could not understand why Tzippi cried incessantly, and this caused him to worry that she would never return to her functioning self or be able to care for their other children. Her tears overwhelmed him and he could not convince her that indeed he cared deeply for their daughter.

Additionally, Moshe began to question his own competency as a griever, and wondered if there was something wrong with him as a result of his limited affective reaction to the loss of his daughter as expected by his wife. This confused Moshe since he felt proud of his efforts to hold down the fort and manage the family. He resented feeling guilty about his own reactions and became more distanced from Tzippi as a result. Through our work the couple was introduced to the notion of different styles of coping with loss and the inherent strengths and weaknesses within each style. This perspective was an eye-opener for them and helped to bridge the growing chasm in their relationship.

Moshe was an instrumental griever. He dealt with loss through action and thrust himself into the activity of organizing study sessions in his daughter's memory and focusing on the ongoing functioning of their other children. Tzippi was an intuitive griever who outwardly expressed emotions and feelings relating to the loss. Their different styles could work to complement each other's approach. They could each learn to appreciate what the other had to contribute, possibly integrating both approaches, rather than feeling threatened by the differences and alienated from each other.

Margaret Stroebe and Hank Shut developed another model of understanding grief responses called the Dual Process Model. It asserts that there are two orientations that comprise the activity of grieving. One is a "loss orientation" in which bereaved individuals struggle with the difficult feelings directly relating to the death, and the other is a "restoration orientation" in which grievers deal with their secondary losses generated by the death. Each orientation has particular stressors and adaptive mechanisms for coping. The loss oriented stressors might include lack of social support and disintegration of future plans with the deceased thus activating concomitant adaptive strategies such as ventilating emotions and looking at pictures. Restoration oriented stressors might include strain on financial resources and the addition of new household obligations thus activating concomitant adaptive strategies such as meeting with a financial planner and hiring help.

This paradigm is helpful in guiding couples who are estranged from each other after a loss because they find their partner's style of coping with the death very incongruous and alien in comparison to their own style to feel a sense of relief that their partner's strategy is 'normal' but contrasting with their own. Stroebe and Shut in fact argue that the most adaptive coping emanates from an oscillation between the two strategies.

Another couple I worked with entered therapy three months after the death of their four-year-old son Shlomo, a death which was preceded by a several-week hospitalization. They decided to begin counseling due to a daily escalation of arguments. Reuven, who worked from home, spent much time rehashing the final weeks of their son's death. He isolated himself and felt that participating in any social activities meant a betrayal of their son. Reuven created a photograph album and spent hours looking at the pictures and talking with his deceased son. He wanted to share these reflective moments with his wife Zahava, a teacher, yet she wanted to participate and be involved in community and family social events as much as possible.

Early sessions focused on exploring their conceptions of a "proper grief response," including looking at how their own nuclear families had grieved losses. Introducing a wider frame for reactions to death via explanation of the Dual Process Model helped Zahava and Reuven develop more compassion for their partner's efforts.

Part of the therapy consisted of helping each spouse role play unexpressed reactions: Reuven was asked to play a more "restorative" role and Zahava more of a "loss role." This assisted them in feeling closer to their partner and mitigated the feeling that they were so out of synch with each other at such a critical time. Research evaluating therapeutic approaches with people suffering loss has shown that there is a greater improvement manifested by either a restorative oriented griever or a loss oriented griever when the intervention encourages the refinement of the coping style that was not their comfortable, preferred style when they came for treatment and support. This further validates the notion that oscillating between both approaches is most therapeutic.

RESPONSES TO SHATTERED ASSUMPTIONS

Anger. Anger management is an issue that troubles many couples that enter therapy even without child loss, and becomes exacerbated following the death of a child. The unnatural death of a child is an event that challenges our basic sense of the world as being a predictable place with rules that govern it, give it meaning, and make it safe.

Angry feelings are a normal response to the temporary breakdown of these basic beliefs. However, these normal angry, indignant, feelings combined with a sense of injustice at the death being undeserved and senseless tug at the fabric of even the most healthy relationships. Often, one person in the couple manifests these emotions by repeating their sense of outrage in a perseverative manner. This person searches for a way to make sense of what happened, either by blaming the doctor, a nurse, the hospital, *Hatzalah*, their spouse, or themselves. Since this is truly an existential dilemma, usually with no clear answer, rational arguments offered by the spouse or a demeaning of the angst that is being expressed meets with more fury and a further sense of irritation, helplessness, and aloneness.

A couple that came to see me after a stillbirth evidenced this predicament. During her last week of pregnancy Tova would wake up sweating and panting from dreams that she was suffocating. Her doctor's visits determined that she and the fetus were fine and that she was just anxious. Two days later she went into labor, went to the hospital, was monitored, and told that the baby had died. She delivered a baby with its cord wrapped around its neck. There was no consoling her.

This traumatic life-wrenching event shook the very foundations of Tova's sense of trust in herself and the medical establishment. Tova, who had struggled with anger issues her whole life following her parents' divorce and her father's subsequent abandonment of the family, displayed an intense fury at her doctor. In order to make sense of this unfathomable situation her husband, Avi, offered to try and sue the doctors. This strategy was not useful for Tova and she was desperate to have her feelings validated. When Avi tried to take an action-oriented approach rather than just offer support she became extremely irritable and bitter towards him. Tova began to blame Avi for the death, accusing him of not taking her dreams seriously enough and being remiss in not forcing the doctors to intervene by having her wear a monitor.

We can immediately recognize that Tova and Avi fell into the categories of intuitive versus instrumental griever. However, it was apparent that Avi lacked the tools to communicate with his wife in a way that she felt supported and understood. She needed him to mirror her feelings and not try and 'fix' the situation. Tova thirsted for support for her underlying feelings of helplessness and urgent reassurance that her perception of the world "was not crazy."

A secondary issue that manifested itself in this couple, which is specific to the situation of miscarriage, stillbirth, or the death of a newborn, is the possible difference in attachment the two parents felt toward the child and its effect on the subsequent grief reaction. Avi only mildly felt that he had lost a child; he was upset for a brief time and was ready to move on and try to have another. In sessions, Tova would try to convince Avi of the terrible loss. She described the conundrum of having giving birth to life and death. Her body felt like she had given birth to a viable baby. Her hormones were those of a mother, her breasts were filled with milk, and she had experienced the baby kicking and vibrant inside of her singing to it, and massaging it. She could not reconcile herself to the fact that her baby was born dead.

Improving their communication skills by encouraging Avi to mirror Tova's feelings, rather than convince her out of her feelings or give her advice, had an enormous positive impact. She felt cared for, supported, and less alone. Similarly, Tova was able to embrace the fact that perhaps Avi was more resilient initially than she was, had different coping strategies, and perhaps he may not have bonded with the baby the way she had, which was a neutral fact based on the physiology of childbirth. This shift in perspective on her part helped him feel less accused and more understood.

Once Tova began to feel less anger at God, the system, and Avi, she began to feel more self-blame, guilt and shame. Her guilt reaction is also one of many normal reactions grievers experience. "I should have insisted they monitor me," "Why didn't I listen to myself and my dreams," "I knew it, and I didn't take care of my baby," "What an incompetent mother I am and would be; I don't deserve a baby." In Tova's situation, the trauma irritated latent self-esteem issues that were lurking there all along but now manifested as terrible self-loathing and marital dissention that Avi could not resolve. It was necessary to disentangle personal unresolved long term issues from the trauma at hand. Once this became clear, Avi felt a sense of relief and was able to hold Tova's hand and soothe her while she grappled with guilt relating to the tragedy and then attend to her own inadequacy issues that stemmed from her early abandonment experiences.

SPIRITUAL OR RELIGIOUS ATTITUDES AND INJUSTICE

Another factor that can be a uniting influence within a couple or might exacerbate underlying issues is the spiritual or religious attitude regarding the death. There are a number of authentic religious perspectives that can be adopted. One parent may approach the loss as *"Hashem's Will,"* believing that it happened for a reason. This person often will try and make the loss a meaningful experience and consequently will embrace a more devout religious lifestyle. A second approach might be the person who exclaims that "this is unjust and unfair. Why did this happen; this is unfathomable and I will never accept it, and I reject religion." A third approach is the parent who says: "I must learn to live with it, forgive, there is no explanation and I must go on," thereby separating the loss from affecting the person's religious and spiritual commitment.

I have seen many couples where their previously shared approach to spirituality and religion, which was a comfort, shared value, and positive overarching framework to their lives, became a point of contention. David could not reconcile the death of his seven-year-old son to leukemia with his assumptive world that believed that there is an order and predictability to the world, and that events happen for a reason. He saw the loss of his child as proof that he and his wife needed to atone for something, correct their behavior, and become more religious. David changed his lifestyle greatly by making many pilgrimages abroad to visit the graves of *Tzaddikim* and accused his wife of being the cause of future losses if she did not join him in his religious fervor and actions. Sarah felt judged, blamed, alienated, controlled, and painfully distant from David. She felt that she not only lost her child but also her partner with whom she shared a life perspective and journey. A former source of joy in their lives became a nexus of dissention and struggle. They discovered that they each held different assumptions about the world.

Some studies have found that people with spiritual beliefs appear to cope better with loss than people with no spiritual beliefs at all. However, Sarah and David were miles apart. Both were high functioning, very successful lawyers who faced the potential shattering of their assumptive worlds in very different ways. Often in situations such as these, in which couples become stuck and experience difficulty in making progress in understanding each other and making room for a variety of grief responses, it becomes important to consider whether old issues are being triggered from each individual's nuclear family.

David experienced Sarah as being unloving when she refused to change in the manner he was demanding. Further exploration over several months revealed that David was replicating a family pattern where in exchange for religious fervor he was rewarded with love. In addition, he was taught that *Hashem* intervenes directly and for every action there is an immediate consequence positive and negative. This approach conflicted with Sarah's upbringing that believed in a benevolent world and divinely transcendent God, but it did not view these kinds of tragedies as cause and effect related, but rather incomprehensible. The couple is continuing to work on being able to embrace differences and express disappointed, angry, confusing feelings and still feel loved, as well as not view an approach different from one's own as unloving, rejecting, irreligious, and abandoning.

CONTINUING BONDS

The paradigm of "continuing bonds" understands parental grief as a continuing, life-long, evolving process. Research has shown that the grief becomes a profound connection between parent and child, developing into an integrated part of their identities and lives. This seems to be true regardless of the years since the death, the age of the child at the time of death, or the cause of death. Bereaved parents feel united with each other by an experience that is comprehended only within their individual relationships and is very hard to communicate to others. (This might possibly explain Aaron's silence.)

Parents appear to develop a connection to the deceased in their hearts with free-flowing access to images and ongoing memories that exist under the surface which are both painful and consoling. Indeed, many grieving parents have described the image of a 'hollow or empty space inside.' There are many other images that are consoling: an empty place at the table, a teddy bear, holding the child, a hole in the fabric of life, a light, saying good night to a photograph, remembering kissing the head of the child.

The bond with the child is not broken, and it is integrated in a new way, allowing for a connection to be maintained with the child. This is best achieved by being a part of a community that is aware of the death, that supported the parent, and that can continue to share in the loss. This very book with its poignant vignettes about loss serves this very purpose.

POSTTRAUMATIC GROWTH AND SUPPORT

I have enumerated and explored many instances where intimacy and communication might break down following the loss of a child. Marital challenges following the trauma of a child's death are to be expected. Healthy couples might also benefit from counseling with a trained professional or participating in a support group following a loss. This might provide a safe place to learn how to identify potential problems, receive reassurance when frightened by their own responses or those of their spouse, and accelerate the healing process. Often, there can be life-transforming growth, enhanced relationships, and new meaningful behavior and attitudes that can emerge from these efforts that strengthen the bond between the couple.

Researchers have intensively studied the concept of "posttraumatic growth," namely, the positive lessons learned from struggling with a major loss or trauma. They posit that this kind of growth occurs in three major areas: a changed sense of self, changed relationships, and a changed philosophy of life. They underscore that this growth is concomitant with significant distress and people who do grow acknowledge both the positive and negative aspects of their experiences.

Due to the shattering of the assumptive world, where the stability and predictability regarding the world has been breached, finding a sense of purpose and meaning in life can provide a healing effect in regaining a sense of comfort and contentment. There is often a renewed sense of purpose, making each moment count and finding each day a blessing. Parents find themselves helping other grieving parents and reassuring them that their feelings are normal. They may find new jobs or get involved in a meaningful project. Others become involved in community or religious activities and have more of a sense of what is important. Parents work on their own relationships and might become better parents if they are blessed with other children. Some describe a renewed faith and a transforming nature of their grief that allows for more compassion. Parents who succeed in developing in this fashion do so despite the trauma that has occured. Nonetheless, sudden temporary upsurges of grief may continue to appear for the duration of their lives.

As mentioned at the beginning of this article the Torah does not describe Adam and Eve's reaction when their son Abel dies. The following legend is recorded of Adam and Eve leaving the Garden of Eden. We can read it as a beautiful metaphor and paradigm that gives us a window into how humankind can go on living and weave loss into one's life and find new meaning.

> Seeing that he would be banished, Adam began to weep again and implored the angels to grant him at least permission to take sweet scented spices with him out of Paradise. . . . The angels implored the Lord on his behalf, and He heard their prayer. . . . Adam gathered . . . all sorts of seeds for his sustenance. Laden with these, Adam and Eve came upon the earth.

Adam and Eve bring spices, something relating to the sense of smell, something ethereal, out of the Garden. They have lost the Garden but they take with them an essence of the Garden which sustains them. They take seeds which can be planted and grow over time. Parents are forever changed by their loss. May they all be blessed to be *ezer ki-negdo* – a helpmate, embracing the unique perspectives, qualities, and characteristics that each brings to the relationship to help negotiate the new Earth that has been bequeathed to them and discover new forms of growth in the process.

A Physician's Perspective

Benjamin W. Corn

AS AN ONCOLOGIST – a physician who specializes in the treatment of cancer – I encounter no greater challenge than those terrible moments when I must tell one of my patients that the medical field can do nothing more to keep them alive. Telling someone that they will die is the make-or-break moment in the dynamic between the doctor and his patient. This is the point in time when I will either earn or lose the trust that I have worked so hard to build in this precious relationship. The dramatic encounter is always stressful and always sacred.

Throughout my career, I have particularly dreaded that moment in caring for a young person stricken with cancer. Indeed, when someone asks what possessed me to become an oncologist, I can disarm any inquiry only until the topic drifts to children or adolescents. There, my defenses neutralize because I, too, ask philosophical questions about justice, and I too feel like turning in my religious credentials, pointing my finger in the direction of theodicy, and throwing my hands in the air to entreat, "What dear God happened to the presumed natural order of the world that You created?!"

Yet there is another element of difficulty in treating young patients. Physicians must also care for the parents, and parents have rudimentary instinct to protect their children. The laudable tendency can interrupt or even interfere with direct communication between doctor and patient. Sometimes physicians are not cognizant of this subtext. Sometimes physicians themselves can subconsciously foster this problem.

One particular case comes to mind, and I am indebted to the family for permitting me to recount the details. At the age of eighteen, Tali was diagnosed with a very rare and aggressive tumor of the brain known as "anaplastic ependymoma." During her service in an elite army unit of the Israel Defense Forces, she experienced several seizures, each preceded by headache. The workup progressed quickly, and before long, magnetic resonance imaging (MRI) showed an ugly mass in the frontal lobes. The neurosurgeon could not remove the tumor in its entirety; therefore, other interventions were needed.

Tali had a unique personality, a unique energy. She possessed physical and emotional strength. Those traits, coupled with her discipline, served her well in a typical day that consisted of a swim at 5 a.m. followed by a full palate of advanced courses at school, then rehearsals to sharpen the music skills that had won her status as a prodigy and recruitment as guest clarinetist by the symphony of her small town in northern Israel.

Tali's iron will left no room for vacillation when she was presented with options for cancer treatment. It was natural for her to assume the role of warrior in her active battle against her tumor. So at every turn, Tali opted for the most aggressive therapies. For instance, she consistently chose the higher doses of radiation and insisted on receiving untested experimental drugs.

Remarkably, as the storm of illness raged, a persistent sense of tranquility surrounded my special patient. Her room in our cancer center felt more like the den of a comfortable home. There were always visitors. There were photographs of loved ones and drawings of pet dogs and cats as well as homemade get-well cards from friends hanging on walls, ceilings and every other surface that would accommodate tape or string. Often when I would enter her room on my rounds, I would do a double-take, not sure that she hadn't installed a cozy fireplace.

Despite the most advanced treatment modern medicine had to offer, Tali's tumor recurred, both in her brain and elsewhere, so that there was immediate need to have a heart-to-heart talk. But with whom to talk? I took the coward's way out. I reviewed the available options in painstaking detail with her father. As the conversation unfolded, it became clear to him that the prognosis was bleak and that we were veering off into a discussion of *kover et beno*; the Talmudic phrase for the macabre scenario of parents burying their offspring. And it became apparent to both of us that the correct thing to do was to bring Tali into the decision-making process. Fortunately, I was reminded that it was my job to speak to his daughter, so the scenario was by no means a case of parent trying to interfere in doctor-patient dynamics. Rather, here was a situation where the doctor had invited interference in hope of easing his difficult task.

The next morning, I arrived early to speak with Tali. In the background, I could hear the interns drawing blood for daily tests and the clanging of breakfast trays being assembled by orderlies who were dispatched from the kitchen. When I entered Tali's room, she beckoned me to have a seat in the big blue reclining chair by the edge of her bed. This was helpful since I make a point of conducting bedside conversations while sitting down. This prevents me from giving a lecture and enables a dialogue to take shape. "You have something to say, don't you doctor?" I nodded and began, "Tali, I'm not the first person to tell you how special you are and how you have brightened up this oncology ward ever since your arrival. The whole staff has been moved by your will to fight and your exuberance. But right now, we have a problem because your tumor is also a crafty fighter, and we've exhausted not all – but most – of the ammunition we have to hurl at it."

As a rising star in the IDF, Tali appreciated my military metaphors. As an exceedingly intelligent human being, before I could finish my explanation, she put two and two together and even took *my hands*. "You're telling me what I know inside, doc. You're informing me that the Angel of Death is circling around my head." Once again, I nodded, this time to acknowledge the jarring existential reality that we faced.

Overall, Tali absorbed the news unbowed, yet there was an endearing quality to her reaction. You could still palpate her strength, but for the first time you couldn't help but notice her vulnerability. She expressed fears about her own mortality and worry about how her parents would pick up the pieces if she were to die at such a young age. Then, in true Tali fashion, she moved on to contemplate only forward progress. She was willing to endure re-treatment despite her understanding that it could bring severe damage to her cognitive function. "At least with your poisons I'll have a chance of beating this thing," she reasoned, "whereas if I leave the tumor unchecked, then surely it will get the better of my IQ anyway." From that perspective she was right. There was nothing to lose.

Before we could succeed in treating the wild spread of menacing tumor cells to her spinal cord, however, Tali lost her battle with cancer. We, who had surrounded Tali, felt devastated. Her father saw most of her characteristics in himself, so as she died, he felt some of himself dying with her. He wanted Tali to live on through the things he would continue to do in life. Accordingly, he re-dedicated himself to activities that would perpetuate her values. In that way, he helped Tali to pass on something of herself to the future. In one of his quests to uncover meaning, he enlisted as a home hospice volunteer with Life's Door – *Tishkofet*, an organization founded by my wife Dvora (a family therapist) and myself. In that work, he rushes to emphasize, "I am not a healthcare professional, yet I know somehow that the mere presence of someone with my experience can provide a lot to the people who will *let me in* to offer spiritual support. I know that I can quietly teach by example and guide those who are suffering towards a stage of understanding."

His words resonated for me. I cannot say that I harbored proverbial feelings of failure, since I was well aware of the grim statistics associated with Tali's malignancy. However, I was moved by this case. An outlet for the father's emotional turmoil had been identified. His resolve to re-direct his feelings through productive channels was invigorating for me as a physician since many in his place would choose to wallow in self-pity. It might not be intuitive to patients and family members, but physicians too are profoundly impacted by the ordeals of those for whom they care.

I became a physician because I thought I heard a calling to heal. Does losing a patient to the disease I am asked to treat constitute failure? For some of my colleagues this is the case and, in turn, they are unable to visit a *shivah* home to comfort a family grieving for their loved one (i.e., the doctor's patient). For me, I have failed when I am unable to help patients and family members broaden their definition of hope beyond the narrow equation of Hope = Cure. When I ask my patient to fight, it is not necessarily to do battle with every malignant cell. Rather, it is to actively create goals that could instill purpose in their life even if that life is measurable in limited time frames. If patients can find meaning in this struggle, can I fail to grow from this encounter?

With this in mind, my wife and I founded Life's Door – *Tishkofet*, an organization for professionals and laymen who seek help in navigating the journey of illness. The organization posits that hope can emerge when there is willingness to deal openly with illness. It is with the recognition that people are capable of changing and even growing when confronting disease that Life's Door – *Tishkofet* offers workshops, retreats, home hospice services and supportive seminars. Ironically, participants in these innovative programs usually take away a new perspective on life. Contending with illness and even death is surely a disquieting proposition; however, if we are intellectually honest and capable of simply being present (as opposed to evading these harsh realities) we will often find that we are touched in new ways as human beings.

What possessed me to go into the field of oncology? There are many answers, but even with tragic deaths of young patients, my decision draws continuing reinforcement from the strength and inspiration of the heroic people whom my profession allows me to try to help.

The Role of the Rabbi in Dealing with Infant Death

Seth Farber

OR PURPOSES OF THIS essay, a rabbi can be anyone whom the family identifies as a rabbinical figure. It might be a rabbi or educator in a school, and it might be someone who does not have formal ordination but is viewed as a knowledgeable person. In my experience, I have served as the "rabbi" when I was a former teacher of parents who subsequently experienced a loss, a congregational rabbi of another set of parents, and simply a friend to another family. In a number of circumstances, through my work at ITIM: The Jewish-Life Information Center, I didn't know the family at all, but was simply called to help.

Some seven months after receiving my rabbinic ordination, I found myself in the basement of a hospital carrying a small box with a deceased infant into my car. Since there were few protocols, at least back then in America, regulating the transfer of the body to a funeral home or how to arrange for a funeral, the baby – following the parents' decision to forego any form of autopsy – was released to me, the ad-hoc family rabbi who was supposed to "take over" from here.

Though the death of the particular infant was a scientific given from even before birth, there was little time to prepare for any sort of service or funeral. The hours following my long walk down the hospital corridor are a blur in my memory, but I do remember that following the funeral, I got back into my car, pulled out of the parking lot (away from the parents' sights), and spent a good half hour on the side of the road crying.

No training could have prepared me (I was twenty-three at the time) for this kind of lonely moment. I use my personal experience as an introduction to this essay because in the end, I feel strongly that the rabbi's role in addressing the death of an infant (and perhaps the days and weeks before the death of an infant when such is a foregone conclusion) will depend to a large extent on the rabbi's personality and character strengths and weaknesses. I have no particular credentials to enable me to provide a rigorous approach to the role of the rabbi, but rather, a certain set of experiences having helped families over the last two decades. My experience in this area has been in both Israel and in North America, though I believe that my comments below cross international borders.

THE RABBI AS INFORMATION PROVIDER

The rabbi's first role is a source of essential information. The discrepancy between a rabbi's knowledge base and the expectations of him is irrelevant. From the moment that a family is made aware of a critical situation, the rabbi may be in a position to help. Particularly in delicate situations that may lead to infant death, the rabbi can play an important role in stabilizing one dimension of the situation. Infant death is a situation where parents lose all control over something that organically, they have complete control over. Providing information, and making clear the directions available to parents and the potential resources accessible can provide a small sense of control to an otherwise unmanageable situation.

The type of information that a rabbi can provide may vary from *halakhic* options available to the family, traditions associated with burial and mourning (especially in the sensitive area of late miscarriages, stillbirths, and deaths of infants less than thirty days old – which traditional Jewish texts treat differently), and practical information related to the coming hours, days and weeks. In Israel, where publishing "death notices" in newspapers is a norm, individuals often turn to rabbis to ask them to help formulate the notice.

Rabbis can help connect a family to the funeral home or *hevra kaddisha* (burial society), and serve as a mediator between the bereaved family and the institutions which the family must encounter.

Since many rabbis have never been exposed to the information packages needed at this sensitive moments, I provide here a few recommendations for rabbis who find themselves in this situation.
1. Don't be afraid to say "I don't know."
2. Cultivate prior to the event a set of contacts and consultants.
3. Expect to be surprised.
4. Be confident in what you can provide.

5. Don't ever overstep your boundaries. You are not a medical professional or a psychologist.

THE RABBI AS INITIATOR

There is a delicate balance between interference and initiative. Taking this into account, the rabbi has a unique role to play in the hours spent dealing with infant death – whether it be in the hospital, the morgue, the *hevra kaddisha*, the burial or the *shivah* house. Parents have no experience with these situations and the rabbi can in many instances, offer assistance by exploring options otherwise unavailable to the family.

Because of the tragic dimensions of infant death, parents often or care providers are in a particularly vulnerable position vis-à-vis authority, and find themselves – in many circumstances – unable to make complex decisions.

I will illustrate this with one of my experiences working with Israeli *hevra kaddishas*. Although in traditional society, parents were discouraged from participating in any form of service for a miscarriage, there are authority figures in certain *hevra kaddishas* who are willing to accommodate parent's requests to know the place of burial, and even to participate in some way in the burial. Today in Israel, for purposes of illustration, the Tel Aviv *hevra kaddisha* (which supervises a number of cemeteries and hospital morgues) has one anonymous communal grave for all infants and miscarriages which is not made known to the public, whereas one of Jerusalem *hevra kaddishas* maintains a defined and marked area which can be accessed.

A family that insists upon knowing the place of the burial will encounter significant opposition in Tel Aviv. They will be told that "it is bad for them to know where the place of burial is," and that they must "move on." Now, I generally do not like to determine the psychology of Jewish tradition, nor do I seek to insist that I know best what is good for a family – especially a bereaved one. In a number of cases, I have initiated contacts from Tel Aviv with certain Jerusalem *hevra kaddishas* in order to allow a family to participate – at least partially – in a burial service or put up a tombstone. This kind of effort can be singularly done be the rabbi, who has the wherewithal to remain connected to the family but also to be cool-headed and seek out options in multiple areas that the family would seek out themselves, were they in a position to do so.

Some practical suggestions for rabbis who may find themselves in this role:

1. Sometimes it is better to show up uninvited than to call or text. Don't assume that the family doesn't need you.
2. Don't be afraid to make blind calls. Just being honest and straightforward sometimes takes away the fear of initiating.
3. Explore as many options as possible, but be prepared that the family might be uninterested in any of your efforts.

THE RABBI AS COORDINATOR

Often, the rabbi plays a role of choreographer of these difficult moments, determining – together with the family – issues such as funeral, *kaddish*, *shivah*, and the like. Since these are areas in flux in the *halakhic* system, these areas may place the rabbi in difficult positions. I believe that the operative agenda must be that one is there to serve the family. No one can put himself in the family's shoes at a particular point, and intuition and common sense go very far in helping families address, at least in part, an intolerable situation.

I have served as liaison to the *hevra kaddisha*, liaison to families providing food for the family (or, in a number of cases, liaison to the local take out place to bring food to hospital rooms), driver, and just about everything between – all in my capacity as rabbi. Standing at the moment of such a tragedy, there is no task to small for a rabbi seeking to help a family.

Some suggestions for rabbis:

1. Have a support staff available to help you, so that you can be in the room as much as possible. Recognize that the delicateness of the situation brings out the best in people. Everyone in the family's circle wants help, and you can probably use their assistance.
2. Try to anticipate what the family's needs will be, and take care of them up front.

THE RABBI AS RELIGIOUS PERSONALITY

If you've gotten this far in this short essay, you are probably wondering why this isn't first. My answer is simple. I don't know how to write about this issue. I find it complex at best to provide meaningful and integrity driven religious counsel at these moments. I'm more preoccupied with Eric Clapton's song, written to his son following his tragic death which speculates "Would you know my name, if I saw you in heaven," than many of the rabbinic responses to these kind of tragedies. I once saw a prominent rabbi speak at a funeral of an infant who simply took out a *Tanakh* and read the story of King David losing his son. This was powerful at the time, and still resonates with me, but I think that the best way for the rabbi to bring God back into the lives of a family is by imitating God, rather than by talking about God. "Just as God is compassionate, so to should you be compassionate; just as God comforts the mourner, so to should you comfort the mourner." Thus, the roles I described above are in my estimation religious functions that express the best about our tradition and allow it to be manifest in modern society.

SOME SUGGESTIONS FOR RABBIS

Don't be afraid to talk about the metaphysical, but also, don't succumb to the impulse to provide easy answers to life's biggest questions.

I believe that rabbis still have an important role to play in the lives of families undergoing terrible loss. Rabbis shouldn't be afraid (as maybe I was when I was twenty-three) to cry with the family, but at the same time, they have opportunities to assist people in ways that few others can. Like in all areas of the religious enterprise, there is a mandate to seize those opportunities and make the most out of them, both for oneself and for the family.

Finally, I would like to address myself to parents who are experiencing or whom have experienced a loss. No one can understand what you are going through. Still, sometimes turning to a rabbi can provide an additional dimension of support that can be helpful. A rabbi is not, as I said before, a substitute for a psychologist or a social worker. But they are not simply individuals who know the answer to some *halakhic* problem. They can provide layers of support and communal contacts not readily available from other sources, and often have been involved with other families who have gone through the same experience. Including them in your pain can often help you try to understand that which cannot be understood.

"Just Like All the Boys"

Ari Kahn

MANY YEARS AGO WHEN I was a relatively young yeshiva student I had the opportunity to study with one of the great rabbis of the previous generation. His name was Rabbi Yisrael Zeev Gustman and he may have been one of the greatest rabbis of the twentieth century. He was certainly the greatest "unknown" rabbi: While he fastidiously avoided the limelight and was therefore unfamiliar to the general public, he was well known to connoisseurs of Torah learning.

His meteoric rise from child prodigy to the exalted position of religious judge in the Rabbinical Court of Rabbi Chaim Ozer Grodzinski at around the age of twenty was the stuff of legend – but nonetheless fact. Many years later, I heard Rav Gustman's own modest version of the events leading to this appointment: A singular (brilliant) insight which he shared with his fellow students was later repeated to the visiting Rav Chaim Ozer, who invited the young student to repeat this same insight the following day in his office in Vilna. Unbeknownst to Rav Gustman, the insight clinched an argument in a complex case that had been debated among the judges in Rav Chaim Ozer's court – and allowed a woman to remarry.

One of the judges adjudicating the case in question, Rabbi Meir Bassin, made inquiries about this young man, and soon a marriage was arranged with his daughter Sarah. When Rabbi Bassin passed away before the wedding, Rabbi Gustman was tapped to take his place as rabbi of Shnipishok and to take his seat on the court. Although Rav Gustman claimed that he was simply "in the right place at the right time," it was

---

This article, based on a combination of first-hand knowledge and a composite reconstruction of events as retold to the author, is reprinted from Aish.com.

clear that Rav Bassin and Rav Chaim Ozer had seen greatness in this young man.

While a long, productive career on the outskirts of Vilna could have been anticipated, Jewish life in and around Vilna was obliterated by World War II. Rav Gustman escaped, though not unscathed. He hid among corpses. He hid in caves. He hid in a pig pen. Somehow, he survived.

For me, Rav Gustman was the living link to the Jewish world destroyed by the Nazis. I never had to wonder what a Rav in Vilna before the war looked like, for I had seen Rav Gustman, thirty-five years after the war. At the head of a small yeshiva in the Rechavia section of Jerusalem, Rav Gustman taught a small group of loyal students six days a week. But on Thursdays at noon, the study hall would fill to capacity: Rabbis, intellectuals, religious court judges, a Supreme Court justice and various professors would join along with any and all who sought a high-level Talmud *shiur* (class) that offered a taste of what had been nearly destroyed. When Rav Gustman gave *shiur*, Vilna was once again alive and vibrant.

One of the regular participants was a professor at the Hebrew University, Robert J. (Yisrael) Aumann. Once a promising yeshiva student, he had eventually decided to pursue a career in academia, but made his weekly participation in Rav Gustman's *shiur* part of his schedule, along with many other more or less illustrious residents of Rechavia and Jerusalem.

The year was 1982. Once again, Israel was at war. Soldiers were mobilized, reserve units activated. Among those called to duty was a Reserves soldier, a university student who made his living as a high school teacher: Shlomo Aumann, Professor Yisrael Aumann's son. On the eve of the 19th of Sivan, in particularly fierce combat, Shlomo fell in battle.

Rav Gustman mobilized his yeshiva: All of his students joined him in performing the *mitzvah* of burying the dead. At the cemetery, Rav Gustman was agitated: He surveyed the rows of graves of the young men, soldiers who died defending the Land. On the way back from the cemetery, Rav Gustman turned to another passenger in the car and said, "They are all holy." Another passenger questioned the rabbi: "Even the non-religious soldiers?" Rav Gustman replied: "Every single one of them." He then turned to the driver and said, "Take me to Professor Aumann's home."

The family had just returned from the cemetery and would now begin the week of *shivah* – mourning for their son, brother, husband and father.

(Shlomo was married and had one child. His widow, Shlomit, gave birth to their second daughter shortly after he was killed.)

Rav Gustman entered and asked to sit next to Professor Aumann, who said: "Rabbi, I so appreciate your coming to the cemetery, but now is time for you to return to your Yeshivah." Rav Gustman spoke, first in Yiddish and then in Hebrew, so that all those assembled would understand:

"I am sure that you don't know this, but I had a son named Meir. He was a beautiful child. He was taken from my arms and executed. I escaped. I later bartered my child's shoes so that we would have food, but I was never able to eat the food – I gave it away to others. My Meir is a *kadosh* – he is holy – he and all the six million who perished are holy."

Rav Gustman then added: "I will tell you what is transpiring now in the World of Truth in *Gan Eden* – in Heaven. My Meir is welcoming your Shlomo into the *minyan* and is saying to him 'I died because I am a Jew, but I wasn't able to save anyone else. But you – Shlomo, you died defending the Jewish People and the Land of Israel.' My Meir is a *kadosh*, he is holy – but your Shlomo is a *Sheliah Tzibbur* – a Cantor in that holy, heavenly *minyan*."

Rav Gustman continued: "I never had the opportunity to sit *shivah* for my Meir; let me sit here with you just a little longer."

Professor Aumann replied, "I thought I could never be comforted, but Rebbi, you have comforted me."

Rav Gustman did not allow his painful memories to control his life. He found solace in his students, his daughter, his grandchildren, and in every Jewish child. He and his wife would attend an annual parade on *Yom Yerushalayim* where children would march on Jerusalem in song and dance. A rabbi who happened upon them one year asked the Rabbi why he spent his valuable time in such a frivolous activity. Rav Gustman explained, "We who saw a generation of children die will take pleasure in a generation of children who sing and dance in these streets."

A student once implored Rav Gustman to share his memories of the ghetto and the war more publicly and more frequently. He asked him to tell people about his son, about his son's shoes, to which the Rav replied, "I can't, but I think about those shoes every day of my life. I see them every night before I go to sleep."

On the 28th of Sivan 5751 (1991), Rav Gustman passed away. Thousands marched through the streets of Jerusalem accompanying Rav Gustman on his final journey. As night fell on the 29th of Sivan, nine years after Shlomo Aumann fell in battle, Rav Gustman was buried on the Mount of Olives. I am sure that upon entering Heaven he was reunited with his wife, his teachers and his son Meir. I am also sure that Shlomo Aumann and all the other holy soldiers who died defending the People and the Land of Israel were there to greet this extraordinary Rabbi. May it be the will of God that the People of Israel sanctify His Name by living lives of holiness which will serve as a light to the nations – and may no more children, soldiers or yeshiva students ever need to join that holy *minyan* in Heaven.

On December 10th 2005, Professor Robert J. Aumann was awarded the Nobel Prize in economics. I am sure he took with him to Stockholm memories of his late wife Esther and his son Shlomo. I suspect he also took memories of his Rabbi, Rav Gustman.

The last time I saw Rav Gustman, I was walking in the Meah Shearim/ Geulah section of Jerusalem with my wife and oldest son who was being pushed in a stroller. It was Friday morning and we saw the *Rosh Yeshivah*, and we said hello and wished him, "Good Shabbos." Then I did something I rarely do: I asked him to bless my son. Rav Gustman looked at the toddler, smiled and said, "May he be a boy like all the other boys."

At first, my wife and I were stunned; what kind of blessing was this? We expected a blessing that the boy grow to be a *tzaddik* – a righteous man – or that he be a *talmid hakham* – a Torah scholar. But no, he blessed him that he should be "like all the boys."

It took many years for this beautiful blessing to make sense to us. The blessing was that he should have a normal childhood, that he have a normal life, that he have his health. Looking back, I realize what a tremendous blessing Rav Gustman gave, and why.

Today, that son – Matityahu – and our second son, Hillel, are soldiers in combat units in the Israeli Defense Forces. Brave, strong, motivated and idealistic, they are wonderful soldiers, wonderful Jews. I pray that they return home safely along with all their comrades, and live normal lives – "just like all the boys."

Editors and Contributors

RABBI JEFFREY SAKS is the founding director of ATID – The Academy for Torah Initiatives and Directions in Jewish Education and its WebYeshiva.org program. He edited *Wisdom From All My Teachers: Challenges and Initiatives in Contemporary Torah Education*, authored *Spiritualizing Halakhic Education*, and is an editorial board member of the journal *Tradition*.

DR. JOEL B. WOLOWELSKY is Dean of the Faculty at the Yeshivah of Flatbush in Brooklyn, NY. He is Associate Editor of *Tradition* and the series *MeOtzar HoRav: Selected Writings of Rabbi Joseph B. Soloveitchik*. His latest book is *The Mind of the Mourner: Individual and Community in Jewish Mourning*.

*

DR. MIRIAM ADAHAN is the author of over 20 books and is an expert on recovery from abuse. She teaches parenting education and how to achieve mental health.

BRIGITTE DAYAN AFILALO, a native of Paris, is a Jewish educator, writer and community volunteer. She lives in Manhattan with her husband, Ari, and their children, Liora and Rami.

DR. MIRIAM BENHAIM is a clinical psychologist with a practice specializing in couple, family and individual psychotherapy. She is Clinical Director of the Center for Loss and Renewal, a group practice specializing in life transition therapy and loss-related issues, and she runs a Process Group for Yeshivat Maharat.

ROOKIE BILLET is the principal of the Shulamith School for Girls Middle Division, having served as a classroom teacher, Yeshiva High School principal, rebbetzin, adult education lecturer, informal educator, and kallah teacher over a career that spans several decades.

RABBI SHALOM CARMY is co-chair, Jewish Studies Executive at Yeshiva College where he teaches Jewish Studies and Philosophy, and is the Editor of *Tradition*.

DR. BENJAMIN W. CORN is Professor of Oncology at Tel Aviv University School of Medicine and Chairman of the Institute of Radiotherapy at Tel Aviv Medical Center. He was awarded the Israeli President's Citation for Volunteerism in 2011.

RABBI SETH FARBER is the founder and director of ITIM: The Jewish Life Information Center, and the Rabbi of Kehillat Netivot in Raanana, Israel.

RABBI DAVID FINE is the Founder and Dean of the Barkai Center for Practical Rabbinics in Modiin and the facilitator of Jewish Identity in the Matnas (community center) of Modiin.

RABBI ARYEH A. FRIMER is the Ethel and David Resnick Professor of Active Oxygen Chemistry at Bar Ilan University and has written extensively on the status of women in Jewish law.

RABBI STEVEN GOLDSMITH lives with his family in Kfar Haro'eh. He serves as the Rabbi of the Bet Elazraki Childrens' Home in Netanya.

DRS. DAN AND DASSI JACOBSON are psychologists in private practice in Jerusalem and Gush Etzion.

RABBI ARI KAHN, an author and educator, is a senior lecturer at Bar Ilan University. His books *Echoes of Eden* have appeared on Bereshit, Shemot, Vayikra, and soon on Bamidbar.

DR. BERNIE KASTNER is a psychotherapist in private practice in Jerusalem and the author of *Understanding the Afterlife in This Life, Masa*

El HaOr, HaOlam She'aharei, and the soon to be published *Back to the Afterlife.*

DR. CHAIM LICHT is Professor Emeritus of the Department of History at the University of Haifa; he is currently involved in research in the aggadic literature of Jerusalem Talmud.

YONIT ROTHCHILD is a freelance writer living in Efrat, Israel. She is the former rebbetzin of the Highland Lakes Beit David Shul in Miami, Florida.

RABBI JOSEPH B. SOLOVEITCHIK זצ"ל, Rosh HaYeshiva at Yeshiva University's Rabbi Isaac Elchanan Theological Seminary, was the preeminent Jewish theologian and Talmudic scholar of the previous century.

RABBI TZVI HERSH WEINREB, Ph.D., is Executive Vice President, Emeritus of the Orthodox Union.

RABBI AVRAHAM (AVIE) WALFISH teaches Jewish studies at Herzog College and Michlala Jerusalem. He received his rabbinic ordination in Israel in 1989 and holds academic degrees from Yeshiva University and Hebrew University.

RABBI AVRAHAM (AVI) WEISS is founder of Yeshivat Chovevei Torah and Yeshivat Maharat in New York, and the senior Rabbi of the Hebrew Institute of Riverdale. His new book, *Holistic Prayer: A Guide to Jewish Spirituality,* is scheduled to be published by Maggid in the summer of 2013.

DR. DEVORA KASACHKOFF WOHLGELERNTER ע"ה was a Bible scholar, Professor of Mathematics, Rebbetzin, and mother of seven. After becoming sick with cancer and losing a child, she made aliya and became a psychotherapist in Jerusalem.